SHOTS
and shooters

SHOTS
and shooters

Maria Costantino

Published by SILVERDALE BOOKS
An imprint of Bookmart Ltd
Registered number 2372865
Trading as Bookmart Ltd
Blaby Road
Wigston
Leicester LE18 4SE

© 2005 D&S Books Ltd

D&S Books Ltd
Kerswell,
Parkham Ash, Bideford
Devon, England
EX39 5PR

e-mail us at:- enquiries@d-sbooks.co.uk

This edition printed 2005

ISBN 1-84509-276-7

DS0098. Shots & shooters

Creative Director: Sarah King
Editor: Debbie Key
Project editor: Nicola Barber
Designer: Debbie Fisher
Photographer: Paul Forrester

Font: Gill Sans

Printed in China

1 3 5 7 9 10 8 6 4 2

Contents

Introduction

In the old Hollywood Western movies, cowboys and outlaws swung by the saloon and downed a shot of whiskey or two fingers (two ounces) in one swallow. Since then, shots or shooters, tooters and slammers have been made with a huge range of wonderful spirits and mixers in bright, colourful concoctions with the most outrageous names and decorated with miniature garnishes.

Shooters not only taste good, they can also be made up in large batches rather than in individual servings, saving you time to enjoy them with friends at a party or celebration. Popular in many bars, bartenders have gone to great lengths to develop exciting new flavours in shooters as well as themed drinks for special occasions. You can serve shooters in shot glasses and there is a huge range of styles available, including novelty shots in the shape of cowboy boots or wild animals. You can even get your own shot glass attached to a necklace! Tooters are a new departure: in some bars these are served in glasses that look remarkably like laboratory test tubes and are held in a rack, while in some kitsch Western-themed bars, staff carry tooters in holsters that look a little like the gun belts worn by cowboys in the movies, but in place of bullets are the tooter tubes.

Frequently the spirit, or lower-proof liqueur, is also combined with one or more juices and the small size of the drinks themselves limits the amount of alcohol contained in each drink. However, in some cases, shooters can be pretty hard stuff! You will find a range of recipes in this book to suit both preferences.

Some of the drinks on offer in this book are technically known among bartenders as pousse-cafés or after-coffees. A pousse-café is more a style of presentation than a class of drink, as there are no common components, although drinks have been served in this style for centuries. Served after dinner, these cocktails consist of several liqueurs or spirits of specific gravities that sit in layers in the glass. The liqueur layers should strictly remain separated, one above the other, although it does take practice and a steady hand to get them absolutely perfect! Each liquor has a different density: basically syrups are heavier than liqueurs, and spirits are lighter. You will need to pour the heaviest density into the glass first, then the next lightest is poured carefully and slowly over the back of a spoon so that it settles in a separate layer, then the next lightest liquor is added.

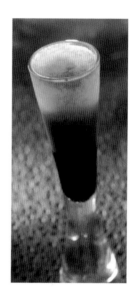

Pousse-cafés usually have at least three layers, but there are some beautiful and delicious drinks to be made with just two layers: it's worth practising with these first to perfect your technique. Pousse-cafés are traditionally served in their own glass: a small, straight-sided, short-stemmed, tube-shaped glass. You could also use a parfait glass or even a cordial glass, sometimes called a pony, which looks like a small white wine glass, but the top has a narrower opening than the base of the bowl. Some well-known pousse-cafés like the B-52 can also be served stirred, strained and on the rocks, and you will find suggestions for alternative ways of serving.

Shooters provide a perfect opportunity to be experimental. First, to try out those strange liquors in often very fancy bottles, and secondly, to adapt recipes to suit your own taste. After all, that's how many cocktails, mixed drinks and shooters were devised! The great fun with shooters, and especially jelly shots, is that it gives you an opportunity to break out that interesting looking bottle of stuff you got on holiday! You'll have so much fun that you'll be searching out more and more exotic ingredients for future use!

To get you familiar with shooters, this book is divided into four sections. In the first chapter, Shots in the Dark, you'll find recipes for shots that don't require any skills beyond pouring liquors into a glass! They're so easy to make, you could (almost!) make them blindfolded!

The second chapter, Shaky Shots, is all about shooters made in a cocktail shaker. These shaky shots are also very easy to make, but instead of pouring into a glass, you pour the liquors into a shaker with ice, shake, and then strain the chilled liquor into the shot glass. Shaking with ice is one way of blending the ingredients into a smooth mix. It also increases the volume of the drink because a little water from the melted ice will find its way into each glass. Shaky shots are fun to make and using a shaker allows you to make up a batch of shooters to fill six shot glasses.

In Trick Shots you'll find recipes for 2- and 3-layered shooters, so you can practice your steady hand skills and impress your party guests! You can have great fun with flavour and colour combinations with these shooters, and making them can be a party game in itself! And, if they don't turn out to be perfect examples of poussecafés, it doesn't matter, because you can always mix them up and they'll taste just as good!

You'll find some recipes for party shooters in the Six Shooters chapter, and in this section there are also some recipes for the latest trend in shooters: gelatine shots. Pretty well any cocktail or shooter recipe can be adapted into a jiggelo or jelly shot. You can eat them by squeezing them out of their plastic shot glass, or, if you have set them in glass shots, eat them with a spoon! And if you don't have enough glasses to go round, you can always set the jelly in a shallow dish or tray and cut out jelly shapes with cookie cutters! With jelly shots, you get shots without losing a drop!

If you're throwing a party and are serving shots, there are a few things to remember:

- Shooters generally contain 5.7 cl/2 fl oz of alcoholic mix. A glance at the recipes will tell you which ones are softer because of the addition of fruit juices and mixers, and which ones are harder as they contain more alcohol per shot. Consequently, three shooters per person, four maximum, will be enough to satisfy!

- Shooters are drinks designed to be downed in one, but you may like a drink so much you want to sip it. That's perfectly all right. For those who down in one, make sure there are plenty of glasses of water and fruit juices available as chasers.

- Responsible drinking is the key to enjoyment, health, and safety, both personally, and the safety of others, especially if you are a driver. Do not drink and drive, and never offer 'one for the road'.

- Do not condone or encourage underage drinking. The recipes in this book are intended for adults. There are numerous non-alcoholic fruity syrups that can be used to create delicious blank bullets or mock shots. You will find that these are very popular with many people because they are so tasty. So, be prepared when you entertain to provide them for all your guests!

- Do not push an alcoholic drink onto a guest: if they say no, they mean no. Offer delicious juices and sparkling minerals instead.

- Never, ever, spike anyone's drink: they may be the designated driver that night; be allergic to alcohol; be on medication; have religious beliefs which preclude alcohol, or they may be in recovery.

The Basics

You don't need to be a professional bartender to be able to mix original drinks, but it does help if you have the right tools for the job.

Cocktail shaker
This is an absolute must for the home bar. The standard version is a three-part shaker, known as a Cobbler Shaker, which consists of a beaker (the bottom section which holds the ice and liquors) and strainer (which slots over the neck of the beaker) and a lid. This shaker is very easy to use: add the ice, pour in the liquors, secure the top and cap, shake, unscrew the cap and strain. Cobbler shakers come in a huge variety of sizes and designs, including my favourite, which is the shape of a penguin!

The Boston Shaker is a two-part shaker that consists of a large stainless steel beaker and a crystal glass top which fits inside the beaker. Because the Boston Shaker doesn't have an inbuilt strainer, you have to strain the liquor through a round, stainless-steel Hawthorne Strainer which has an edge that looks a bit like a coiled spring! Using this can be a bit fiddly, but you could always strain the liquor through a tea-strainer!

Long-handled bar spoon
As the name suggests, this is a spoon with a long handle around 25 cm/10 inches long and made of stainless steel. At the end of the handle there is usually a disc called a muddler used to muddle or crush pieces of fruit, herbs or sugar cubes. The bowl of the spoon at the other end holds 1/6 of an ounce of liquid the same amount as a standard teaspoon.

The back of the bowl – the rounded side – is used to make pousse-cafés: the liquor is poured slowly over the back of the spoon. If, however, you find the technique of pouring very slowly hard to handle, cheat! Use a turkey baster to gently drip the liquor over the back of the spoon!

Pony jigger/bar measure
This is one piece of equipment that you really must have. The jigger is made of stainless steel and consists of two cups: a 1 ounce (a pony!) measuring cup at one end, and a 1½ ounce (a jigger!) measuring cup at the other. When you shop for one, look for one with clearly marked ¼-ounce and ½-ounce markings inside the jigger end. As an alternative, you could use a shot glass with markings on it, or a standard set of kitchen measuring spoons 3 teaspoons or 1 tablespoon = ½ ounce; 4 teaspoons = ¾ ounce; and 2 tablespoons = 1 ounce.

A note on parts and measures

In this book you will see that the recipes calls for 1 part, or ½ part of a spirit or liqueur. The word 'part' is used because of the slight variations between metric, British Imperial and US measurements, as each side of the Atlantic has a variation on the fluid ounce. Since most of the classic cocktails were invented in America, the jigger used in bars in the USA is often a common measurement. It really doesn't matter what jigger you use, you could use a shot glass, or even an egg cup (or a bucket!) as your measure. As long as you use the same measure throughout, the ratios of one spirit to another in your drink will be correct.

Shot glasses in general hold around 5.7 cl/2 fl oz, although there are some that are smaller and some that are larger. It's a good idea though to measure, using water, the total quantities of a drink and pour them into the glass to make sure all the contents fit! Don't forget though that shaking with ice will dilute and increase the volume of the finished drink, so you need to allow for this when you measure!

Ice

Many of the shooters in this book are made by being shaken with ice. Around 4-5 ice cubes are needed to mix a drink. Make plenty of cubes up, or buy them ready-frozen and keep them to hand in a good, insulated ice bucket. To stop the cubes sticking together, give them a spray with a dash of soda water! One or two recipes may call for crushed ice, but check first if your blender blades are designed for ice-crushing! Alternatively, put some ice cubes into a plastic bag, or wrap them in a bar cloth and hit them with a rolling pin. Crushed ice melts really quickly, so you'll need quite a few cubes even to fill a shot glass!

Bottle stoppers with pourers

These may seem like a bit of a luxury, but it makes controlling the flow of liquor from a bottle much easier and less wasteful as you'll spill less! Take the cap off a bottle of spirits or liqueurs and pop one in; it will also keep the air out. This is vital with some ingredients such as grenadine (a fruit syrup made from pomegranates) which, if left exposed to the air, will start to ferment! If you prefer, you can decant smaller amounts of liquors into smaller measuring jugs and pour from these.

Glasses

Appearance is as important as taste when you serve someone a drink. Shot glasses come in a range of styles from classic and elegant to kitsch and quirky. The only rule about shot glasses is that if you intend to slam them on the bar, make sure they are strong enough! Always wash them immediately after use to remove traces of sticky liqueurs. Rinse them in clean hot water to remove greasy streaks and dry them with a clean towel. Use a glass towel so bits of lint don't get stuck to your shiny glasses.

Methods

To shake and strain a drink, first fill the shaker half-full with ice cubes. Add the ingredients and shake briskly until you feel the outside of the shaker turn very cold!

Pour the liquid immediately through the strainer, leaving the ice behind. Remember the volume of liquid will have increased as some of the ice will have melted. This is important so you don't produce more mixture than the shot glass will hold! Wrap a cloth around the seal if your shaker is prone to dripping!

Don't shake mixes with fizzy components such as champagne, sparkling wine or sodas. You can shake the other ingredients first, then add the fizzy stuff and stir with your long-handled bar spoon. Then put the strainer back on and pour the mixture into the glass, leaving the ice cubes behind.

Use fresh ice cubes for each batch of drinks and wash out the shaker when you switch to a different recipe. You don't want to spoil the flavour or colour of one drink with ingredients from another!

Sugar syrup and sweet and sour mix
In some recipes you'll find the ingredients call for sugar syrup or sweet and sour mix. Sugar syrup, sometimes called syrup de gomme, is a useful colourless liquid, ideal for adding sweetness to a drink. Because ordinary granulated sugar doesn't dissolve well in cold drinks, bartenders use this ready-made sugar solution.

Sweet and sour is another time-saving mix used in many bars, where recipes requiring lemon juice and sugar syrup are likely to be needed in quantity.

Sugar syrup: Dissolve equal volumes of water and sugar (say, ½ cup water and ½ cup sugar) by simmering gently over a low heat for around two minutes. Allow the mix to cool and then decant it into a handy bottle. You can decant it further into a smaller jug for easy pouring if you wish.

Sweet and sour mix: Blend together ½ egg white, 85g/3oz/½ cup sugar, ¼ litre/9fl oz lemon juice, ¼ litre/9fl oz of water. This will keep refrigerated for up to 3 days. Don't be alarmed at the use of egg white here: yes it's raw, but when it's mixed with alcohol it is effectively cooked.

Jelly shots

The party shots need a little forward planning as you'll need time for them to chill and set in the fridge. Gelatine is available in a variety of forms: quick fruit-flavoured versions, unflavoured gelatine and vegetarian gelatine, all of which are widely available in most supermarkets. In Britain, the range of flavours is limited compared to those available in the United States, where the proprietary brand Jell-o is available in flavours such as cherry, grape, melon, banana, cranberry and kiwi to name just a few. With the popularity of jelly shots, the range available outside the USA is set to grow!

Unflavoured gelatine is great for jelly shots because you have a neutral, flavourless and colourless base to which to add your liquors. To make the flavours more intense, it can help to use half the required amount of hot water needed to dissolve the gelatine, mixed with the spirits/liqueurs to make up the required amount, and then the balance added when the mix is cool. Follow the manufacturer's instructions on the packet: with unflavoured gelatine often you sprinkle the gelatine onto the warmed liquid, rather than adding the liquid to the gelatine!

Whatever brand of gelatine you use, you'll need to do a bit of maths to work out how much to use. Read the instructions on the packet. With flavoured gelatine, one pack will be enough to make around 20fl oz/600ml shots or 10fl oz/300ml shots.

All spirits and liqueurs can be used in gelatine shots, although some do work a bit better than others. In general, the liqueurs that have a cream base, such as Baileys Irish Cream, have a tendency to separate. This may affect the appearance of a jelly shot, but not the flavour. Don't confuse cream liqueurs with those called crème: crème liqueurs often have a fruit as their base, not dairy cream, so they won't separate!

It is perfectly possible to create jelly shots using milk too! Full milk, skimmed or semi-skimmed all work well, and so does soya milk! Using milk with, for example, crème de cacao will make for a creamy shot. In desserts, these creamy confections are called bavarois. All you do with these shots is simply replace the specified quantity of water in which to dissolve the gelatine with milk! Alternatively, you can make up the gelatine, either flavoured or unflavoured, with hot water, add the spirits when cool, and extend the whole mixture into a creamy delight by adding milk or yoghurt for extra thickness! That's the fun with shooters and jiggling jelly-shots, they're yours to have fun with and to create your own delights.

If you like, you can also create multilayered and hence, multicoloured and flavoured jelly shots! All you need to do is to let one layer set in the fridge before you add the next layer. These are delicious, in fact, they make really good adult desserts!

Vital Ingredients

Cocktail barmen and women have been extremely ingenious and exceptionally generous over the years in devising and revealing their recipes. Some of the recipes for drinks in this book specify certain proprietary brands, as this is how they were created. While it is possible to make substitutions, you will find there are subtle and, in some instances, not so subtle differences in flavour! Where possible, try the stated ingredients, and then experiment for yourself. In all cases, to get the best possible flavours out of your shots, use the best-quality ingredients – and that means the freshest juices and mixers. Where a recipe says don't chill beforehand, keep the liquors at room temperature. In other instances, chill the ingredients beforehand.

Some of the ingredients may be familiar to you, some less so, so here's a list with some information about their origins and flavours. The figures expressed as % refer to the abv – alcohol by volume. In the USA, this is expressed as proof. Simply multiply the percentage given by 2 and you'll have the proof. But beware, in different countries, the same brand may have a different abv/proof, so always check the label!

Absinthe (68%): An aniseed flavoured pastis (see below) originally made in Switzerland and containing wormwood. Absinthe was banned in most of Europe in the early 19th century, but it has recently been reintroduced.

Advocaat (17.2%): A brandy-based liqueur from the Netherlands which is sweetened with egg yolks.

Akvavit (Aquavit) (40% or 45%): A grain- or potato-based spirit which is usually flavoured and aromatised with fragrant spices like caraway seeds, fennel, cumin, dill and bitter oranges. The Scandinavian countries and Germany produce the true akvavits which are often called schnapps, a name derived from the old Nordic word *snappen*, meaning to snatch or seize, and denoting the traditional way of drinking down in one gulp! In Denmark, Aalborg produces a premium high-strength (42%) akvavit, while Archers produces a well-known range of less strong (around 23%) fruit-flavoured schnapps.

Amaretto (28%): An almond-flavoured liqueur from Italy, the most famous proprietary brand is Amaretto di Saronno.

Anis (45%): An aniseed-flavour pastis (see below). The most famous proprietary brand is Pernod.

Anisette (30%): A sweet aniseed-flavour liqueur made with anise. The best-known maker is Marie Brizzard.

Applejack (40%): An American apple brandy.

Armagnac (40%): A grape brandy distilled from wines produced in the Armagnac region in France using only specified white wines in three sectors: Haut Armagnac (white), Tenareze and Bas Armagnac (black). If the spirit is described simply as Armagnac it is a blend of these three types.

Baileys Irish Cream (17%): A sweet, cream liqueur (as distinct from a crème liqueur, see below) made with whiskey and cream and flavoured with coffee. Baileys is the most well-known proprietary brand.

Benedictine (40%): A bright, golden and aged liqueur made from a secret recipe of 75 herbs, originally made by Benedictine monks.

Bitters: The term bitters refers to a number of spirits flavoured with bitter herbs and roots. These range from products such as Campari, which can be drunk in whole measures like any other spirit or mixed with other ingredients such as Fernet-Branca, Jagermeister or Amer Picon, to bitters that are added in drops to season a drink. The most famous of these dropping bitters are undoubtedly Angostura Bitters, made from a secret Trinidadian recipe; Peychaud Bitters made in New Orleans; and Abbots Aged Bitters made in Baltimore, Maryland since 1865. There are also orange bitters made by numerous companies.

Bourbon: This is a generic term for a bourbon-style American whiskey, distilled in a continuous still method from fermented cereal mash containing a minimum of 51% corn and aged for 68 years in oak casks.

Brandy and cognac (40%): Both are spirits made from distilled grape wine. Brandy can be made in any country where vines are grown, for example Pisco is a clear brandy from Peru and Chile. Cognac can only come from the Cognac region in France where the brandy is made from white wines and is distilled in traditional pot-stills before maturing in oak casks. Cognacs are labelled: VSO (Very Superior Old) VSOP (Very Superior Old Pale) VVSOP (Very, Very Superior Old Pale) and XO (Extremely Old).

Calvados (40%): An apple brandy made in Normandy, France.

Campari (24%): A bitter, red Italian aperitif wine.

Chambord (16.5%): Black raspberry liqueur from Burgundy, France.

Champagne (12%): A French sparkling wine. True champagne must be made by the champagne method in which the sparkle is made by secondary fermentation in the bottle, not in a vat or by artificially carbonating it. To be called Champagne, it must be made using the prescribed method and be produced in the Champagne region of France, a region about 160 kilometres/100 miles northeast of Paris around the towns of Rheims and Epernay.

Chartreuse, yellow (40%), green (55%): An ancient French liqueur made by Carthusian monks. There are two colours: green Chartreuse which is intensely powerful and aromatic, and yellow Chartreuse, which is sweeter and slightly minty in flavour.

Coconut rum (25%): Rum-based sweet coconut liqueur. The best known brand is Malibu.

Cointreau (40%): Properly speaking, this very popular branded liqueur is a form of curacao (see below), a brandy-based spirit flavoured with the peel of bitter oranges. It can be served straight-up, on the rocks and in mixed drinks, where it is often used in place of Triple Sec (see Curacao).

Crème liqueurs: These are sweetened liqueurs as distinct from dry spirits like whisky or cognac and consist of one dominant flavour, often, but not always, fruit: there are also nut-flavoured liqueurs. The most commonly used crème liqueurs are:

Crème de banane (30%): A sweet clear, yellow banana liqueur. A banana liqueur made from green bananas is Pisang Ambon, a product of Indonesia.

Crème de cacao: Chocolate-flavoured and comes in two varieties: Dark (25%) which is a distillate of cocoa beans and sometimes vanilla, macerated in alcohol, diluted and sweetened, and White (20%) which has a more subtle flavour and is colourless, because the cocoa remains are absent.

Crème de cassis (20%): A blackcurrant-flavoured liqueur.

Crème de fraise (20%): A strawberry-flavoured liqueur.

Crème de framboise (20%): A raspberry-flavoured liqueur.

Crème de menthe (25%): White and green liqueurs distilled from a concentrate of mint leaves. The white version has a more subtle flavour than the green which gets its colour from a colorant.

Curacao: Originally, a white rum-based liqueur flavoured with the peel of bitter green oranges found on the island of Curacao. Today it is made by a number of companies with brandy as the base spirit. A variant name is Triple Sec (30%) (the most famous being Cointreau), but confusingly, curacao is not sec (dry) but always sweet. Curacao comes in a range of colours as well as the clear version: orange, red, yellow, green and blue (30%). Whatever the colour, they all taste of orange and they add a wonderful colour to mixed drinks and cocktails.

Eaux de Vie (Waters of Life): These are spirits produced from fruits other than grapes and apples: they are colourless (because they have not been aged in wooden casks) fruit brandies, most often made from soft berries and fruits like pears (such as Poire William), and cherries (such as Kirsch). Eaux de vie are not sweetened and should not be confused with their syrupy liqueur cousins with the same flavours – but these tend to be coloured anyway!

Frangelico (24%): An Italian wild hazelnut liqueur. It comes in a bottle shaped like a monk!

Galliano (35%): This is a golden yellow liqueur from Italy made to a secret recipe of some 80 herbs, roots and berries, with the principal flavourings being liquorice, anise and vanilla.

Gin (40%): London Dry Gin is made from a distillate of unmalted grain. The spirit is infused with juniper and other botanicals before and during distillation to produce a gin with a subtle flavour and aroma. London Dry Gin is therefore a style of gin and there are many famous brands to choose from such as Gordons, Bombay Sapphire, and Beefeater. Plymouth Gin (37.5%) is made only in Plymouth, England and is the traditional gin used for Pink Gin. This is produced by Coates at the Blackfriars distillery in the city.

Grand Marnier (40%): French cognac-based curacao, made with the juice of Caribbean oranges and cask-aged.

Grenadine: This is a sweet syrup, flavoured with pomegranate juice which gives it a rich, pink colour. It is used to add colour, flavour and sweetness to many cocktails. Grenadine is non-alcoholic, or has a very low alcohol content, so once the bottle is opened, the syrup will start to ferment and mould. Keep it in a cool place, but not in the fridge, as this can cause the sugar to crystallise or harden, which will make it difficult to mix with other ingredients.

Irish whiskey (40%): Similar to Scotch, but the difference here is that the barley is dried in a kiln rather than over a peat fire.

Jack Daniels (40%): A brand of Tennessee sour mash whiskey from Lynchburg, Tennessee.

Jagermeister: A brand of German bitters (see above).

Kahlua (26.5%): A dark-brown coffee-flavoured liqueur from Mexico.

Kummel (38%): A pure grain distillate, effectively a type of vodka in which caraway seeds are infused to produce a spearmint-flavoured liqueur made in Latvia, Poland, Germany, Denmark, the Netherlands and in the USA.

Mandarine Napoleon (40%): This is also a type of curacao (see above), but this time made with skins of tangerines steeped in cognac and other French brandies before being coloured to a vivid yellow-orange with carotene and matured for several months. Mandarine Napoleon, the leading brand, is in fact made in Belgium.

Maraschino (40%): This is a clear, colourless liqueur derived from an infusion of pressed cherries and cherrystone distillate and aged for several years. Originally, Marasca cherries grown in Dalmatia were used, but when this area became part of the Venetian empire, plantings of the Marasca cherry trees were established in the Veneto. A number of Italian companies produce maraschino (pronounced maraskino) including Luxardo (in straw-covered flasks), Drioli and Stock.

Melon liqueur (23-25%): A bright green, sweet and syrupy liqueur, the most famous of which is the Japanese brand Midori. The flavouring agent is melon, but the bright green is achieved through the use of vegetable dyes.

Ouzo (40%): A spirit from Greece distilled with anise seeds.

Pastis (45%): A traditional drink of the Mediterranean countries from Spain to Greece and beyond, where it is known by a variety of names: Pastis is an old French word meaning *pastiche*, a 'mixture' or 'muddle'. Pernod and Ricard are the best-known pastis.

Rum: The distilled spirit of fermented sugar cane sap. The cane is crushed to remove the sap, the water allowed to evaporate off, and the resulting syrup is spun in a centrifuge to separate out the molasses which are extracted, reduced by boiling, then fermented and distilled. The exceptions to this method are rums from Haiti and Martinique which are made from reduced, but otherwise unprocessed, sugar cane sap. Dark rum (40%) is matured for about five years in barrels previously used for bourbon. The rum is then blended and sometimes caramel (burnt sugar) is added to darken the colour. White rum (40%) is a clear, colourless, light-bodied rum: the molasses are fermented then distilled in a column-still to produce the clear spirit which is aged for just one year before bottling. Golden rum (40%) is produced in the same way as white rum, but is aged for around three years in charred barrels which give the rum its golden hue and mellow flavour.

Rye whiskey (40%): Produced in both Canada and the USA, rye is distilled from a mixture of cereals but no less than 51% rye.

Sambuca (42%): This is an Italian aniseed-flavoured liqueur made from anise, herbs and roots. It is available in two versions: golden and Negra (black).

Schnapps (40%): A grain or potato-based spirit sometimes redistilled with flavourings such as peach and cinnamon.

Scotch Whisky (40%): Blended Scotch is a mixture of grain spirit, usually maize and one or more Malt Whisky. The malt whisky is made from barley which has germinated, been dried over smoky peat fires, mashed, fermented, distilled and aged in wooden casks for 10-12 years or more.

Sloe gin (26%): This is not a spirit but a liqueur made of sweetened gin in which the fruit (sloes) of the blackthorn bush have been steeped and then strained out after they have stained the spirit a deep red.

Southern Comfort (40%): Americas foremost liqueur uses American whiskey and peaches in a recipe that is a closely guarded secret. The practice of blending peach juice and whiskey was common in the bars of the southern states of America in the 19th century, and this no doubt played its part in the creation of one of the most popular liqueurs. Unusually for a liqueur, Southern Comfort has a high bottled strength.

Tequila (40%): Tequila is a spirit distilled in the region of the same name in Mexico from the cactus-like plant *agave tequilana* . The heart of the cactus is harvested, steam cooked and crushed to remove the juice which is then fermented and double distilled. Silver tequila is matured briefly in stainless steel or wax-lined vats so it remains colourless and a little coarse. Gold tequila is matured in oak vats for three or more years where it develops a more mellow flavour and a golden colour.

Tia Maria (27%): A dark, sweet, coffee-flavoured liqueur from Jamaica based on dark Jamaican rum that is at least five years old, Blue Mountain coffee and local spices. As well as mixing well in many cocktails, Tia Maria is also popular straight up, or drizzled over chocolate desserts!

Vermouth (15%): The cocktail bar would be nothing without vermouth. There are French vermouths and Italian vermouths, and there are dry and sweet vermouths, as well as white or bianco, rose and rosso vermouths. The best-known brands of dry, white vermouths are Martini from Italy, and Noilly Prat and Lillet from France. Cinzano produce the well-known Bianco vermouth which is sweet. Red vermouths are produced by Cinzano, Martini, and by Carpano, who make Punt e Mes , a deep red bitter vermouth from Turin. Dubonnet from France, which can be either red or white, is also a version of vermouth.

Vodka (40%): This is an almost neutral spirit distilled from a fermented mash of grain which is filtered through charcoal. There are colourless and odourless varieties as well as subtly flavoured and aromatised versions such as Bison Grass vodka, Cherry vodka, Lemon vodka, and Pepper vodka.

Wild Turkey (known as 101) (43% and 50.5%) : A brand of straight Kentucky bourbon.

Shots in the Dark
Quick Shots & Slammers

In this section, all the recipes are very simple to make. In most cases you just have to pour the ingredients into a shot glass, although one or two do make use of really chilled ingredients. In these instances, you can refrigerate the ingredients well in advance, or if you need to chill them down in a hurry, stir or shake them with ice cubes, and then strain the liquor into the glass.

Although the glasses may seem small, a shot glass is about 5.7 cl/ 2 fl oz, so they are nevertheless packed full of alcohol, and two or three shots per person should be plenty! Make sure you have plenty of water, juices and maybe a few beers as well for chasers!

There are plenty of opportunities to try your favourite tipple as well as some interesting liqueurs and spirit combinations in shots. Take a look at the recipes and choose your weapon!

Gin & Beer It

1 part gin • 1 part beer

The pun may be awful, but the drink is very tasty indeed: gin is one of the most popular spirits in cocktails and mixed drinks.

method

Don't pre-chill the gin or beer, just pour them straight into the shot glass.

Amaretto Slammer

I part Amaretto • Splash of lemon-lime soda

A nice introduction to slammers! The trick is to drink the shot before it fizzes over the glass! Amaretto has a delicate almond flavour which is given a little sharpness here by the lemon-lime soda.

method

Put the Amaretto into the shot glass and add the splash of lemon-lime soda. Place a napkin, or clean hand, over the glass. Raise the glass 2 or 3 inches, then rap firmly on the bar or table. Drink quickly while it's still fizzing.

For the classic Tequila Slammer just replace the Amaretto with tequila.

Astronaut Shooter

I part chilled vodka • I lemon wedge • Sugar
Instant coffee powder

You might not expect to find instant coffee in a shooter, but this combination is truly out of this world. Too many, and you'll surely be seeing stars.

method

Coat the lemon wedge on one side with sugar and the other with the powdered instant coffee. Really chill the vodka, shake, not stir it, with some ice, then strain into the shot glass. Suck the lemon and then shoot the vodka.

Don Quixote

1 part Guinness stout • 1 part tequila

In honour of Cervantes' hero, but why not make two: one for Don Quixote and one for his trusty sidekick, Sancho Panza. A couple of these and you'll soon be tilting at windmills too!

method
Don't pre-chill the ingredients, just pour into a shot glass.

Fire Truck

1 part Jagermeister • 1 part ginger ale

A fiery combination that may have you calling the emergency services! Jagermeister is a German 'bitters' with a rich, herby flavour. The name means 'master of the hunt'.

method

Chill the Jagermeister. You can shake or stir it with ice first, then strain into a shot glass. Then pour in the ginger ale. To make a Firetruck with a Siren, add 1 part vodka.

Lemon Drop

1 part spice rum (or citrus vodka) • 1 lemon wedge
1 teaspoon sugar

You may well remember the bittersweet lemon drop sweets you could get as a kid. This is the grown-up version. Which taste nicer? Suck 'em and see!

method

Place the sugar on the lemon, shoot the rum (or vodka) and then suck the lemon.

An alternative, and only for close friends, is called a Body Shot: 1 part vodka; 1 individual packet of sugar; 1 lemon wedge. Pour the sugar onto your friend's neck. Put the lemon wedge skin-side inwards into their mouth. First you lick their sugared neck, then shoot the vodka and finally suck the lemon from their mouth!

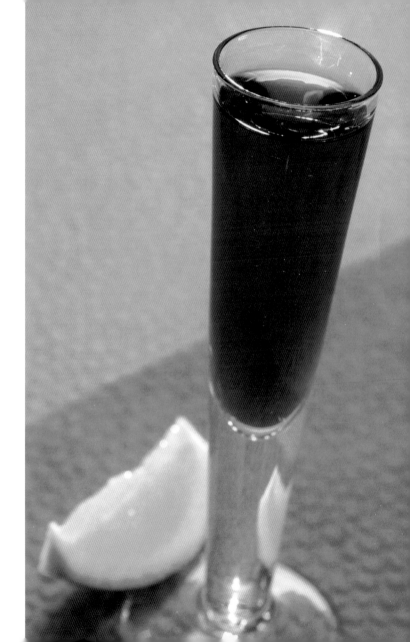

Cordless Screwdriver

1 part vodka • 1 orange wedge • 1 teaspoon sugar

The original long screwdriver appeared in the 1950s and evidently got its name from a US oil man in Iran who stirred his drink with one of his screwdrivers. Try this cordless version!

method

Chill the vodka. You could shake or stir it with ice and then strain into the shot glass. Dip the orange wedge into the sugar. Shoot the vodka and then immediately suck the orange wedge.

For a Rum Screw, replace the vodka with white rum. For a Super Screw use 1 part vodka, 1 part orange juice and 1 part soda water. Pour into a glass neat.

Dr Pepper

1 shot glass Amaretto • ½ glass of beer

Can't manage a whole beer? Try this half-size version then! This drink tastes just like pop, but has more of a kick. Why not try a flaming Dr Pepper? Just add a drop of rum and ignite before dropping the shot into the beer – but take care!

method

Drop the shot glass of Amaretto into the beer and drink before it foams over!

Boiler Maker

One 12-ounce/350ml beer • 1 shot glass of whisk(e)y

This is a classic, but make sure you don't break
your teeth on the shot glass! This drink
originated in the 1920s, when it was a favourite
with big, strong working men!

method

Fill a glass with 12 ounces/350ml of beer and a shot
glass with whisk(e)y of your choice. Hold the shot glass
of whisk(e)y over the beer and gently drop it in.

For a variation on the Boiler Maker, try a Depth Charge
using 1 shot glass of peppermint schnapps.

Dakota

1 part bourbon • 1 part tequila

Two states united in one! An unusual combination of Bourbon whiskey and Mexico's national spirit, tequila, but one that will have you coming back for more.

method

Don't pre-chill the ingredients, just pour them into a shot glass and shoot.

Southern Pepper Slammer

1 part Southern Comfort • 1 part Dr Pepper soda

A delicious, fizzy combination of sweet peach and spicy Dr Pepper. Packs quite a wallop!

method

Don't chill the ingredients, just pour the Southern Comfort into the shot glass and add the Dr Pepper. For a So Co Slammer, use 1 part cola in place of the Dr Pepper.

Dead Bird

1 part Jagermeister • 1 part Wild Turkey

A chance to use Germany's famous bitter, Jagermeister, whose name means 'master of the hunt'. That's why this Wild Turkey, a straight Kentucky bourbon, is a dead bird!

method

Don't chill the ingredients, just pour into the shot glass. Take aim and shoot!

Funky Chicken

1 part Wild Turkey • 1 part tequila

Another bird, another good reason to get the Wild Turkey out! This one will have you dancing around the room!

method

Simply pour the ingredients into the shot glass neat. Don't chill them first. Shoot!

Brain Eraser

1 part vodka • 1 part Amaretto • 1 part coffee liqueur
(Tia Maria or Kahlua) • Dash of soda

This shooter you drink through a straw all at once! You'll almost be able to feel those brain cells floating away.

method

Fill a glass with crushed ice and add the vodka, Amaretto and coffee liqueur. Top with a dash of soda and drink it down all in one go through a straw.

Bandera

1 part lime juice • 1 part tequila • 1 part tomato juice

The word *bandera* is Spanish for 'flag', and the flag in question here is the Mexican flag. A perfect way to celebrate the country's national day on 1st May.

method

Take 3 shot glasses and line them up in front of you. Fill the first glass with lime juice, the second glass with tequila and the third with tomato juice: you now have the three parts of the Mexican flag! Start with the lime juice and shoot them all as fast as you can in that order!

Black Rain

A very smart shot, like a pearl-handled revolver!
Black Sambuca has a licquorice-aniseed flavour with
just a hint of coffee.

method

Pour the Sambuca Negra into the shot glass and add the
chilled champagne.

Manchurian Candidate

1 part chilled vodka • 1 part soy sauce

Watch the movie, catch the remake, try the shot!
Just make sure you don't have too many, as you may
find someone trying to brainwash you!

method

Chill the vodka — you can either shake or stir it with ice
cubes, then strain into the shot glass. Add the soy sauce.
For a Black Samurai, substitute the vodka with 2 parts
sake! Kampai!

T.N.T.

The combination sounds gentle enough: after all, what could be explosive about tonic water? But mixed with tequila, it's pure dynamite!

method

Don't pre-chill the tequila or tonic water. Pour them straight up into the shot glass.

Blood Clot

I part Southern Comfort • Splash of Grenadine

A gruesome name, but it has to be said, this is exactly what it looks like! Don't let the name put you off – it's a very tasty shot!

method

Don't chill the ingredients, just pour the Southern Comfort into the shot glass and add the splash of Grenadine to make the blood clot!

Tablazo

1 part ginger ale • 1 part vodka

What does the name mean? We don't know, but it sounds like a fiery drink, and indeed it is. Put your hand over the glass, slam it on a table and drink it before you lose it!

method

Pour the ingredients straight into a shot glass.

Klondike

1 part Baileys Irish Cream • 1 part Jagermeister

You'll certainly get a rush from this drink. And while it might not make you rich, you'll have a golden glow! Just don't drink too many. You know what they say about fool's gold, and no one wants to be a fool, do they?

method

Pour the ingredients neat into the shot glass.

Orange Crush Shooter

1 part vodka • 1 part Triple Sec/Cointreau
1 part soda water

Orange Crush is a nice, fruity soft drink, perfect for a summer's day. This shooter is a nice fruit drink with a kick! Still perfect for summer though, day or night!

method

Don't pre-chill the ingredients. Pour the vodka and Triple Sec/Cointreau into the shot glass and add the soda.

Jack Hammer

1 part Jack Daniels • 1 part tequila

If you're wondering how this drink got its name, try a couple of them. There, can you feel the pounding in your head? What does it remind you of? Exactly!

method

Pour the Jack Daniels and tequila straight into a shot glass.

Burning Cherry

1 part bourbon • 1 part whiskey • 1 part Scotch
Dash of Grenadine

If whisk(e)y is your poison, this is for you! With 3 different varieties combined, this should probably be called a Smokin' Cherry.

method

Don't pre-chill the ingredients. Pour the whiskies into a shot glass neat and top with the dash of Grenadine. Give a quick stir before slamming.

CHPOK

1 part chilled vodka • 2 parts chilled champagne

Not a misprint but a delicious combination of champagne and vodka. Don't make the mistake of serving this at a wedding reception however. Not unless you want the guests CHPOK-ing all over the place.

method

Get the ingredients really cold beforehand and then pour the vodka into the glass and add the champagne.

Italian Russian

1 part vodka • 1 part Sambuca

Could be an Italov or a Russital. The chill of the vodka, mixed with the heat of the Sambuca will make everyone seem like a comrade.

method

Pour the ingredients straight into a shot glass. Don't pre-chill the ingredients.

Dirty Rotten Scoundrel

1 part vodka • 1 part melon liqueur

Bad day at the office? Boss getting you down? Forget it all with one of these! The satisfaction you'll get from pounding this shot on the table will relieve all your frustrations.

method

Don't chill the vodka or melon liqueur, just pour into a shot glass.

Malibu Cola

1 part Malibu • 1 part cola

How easy can a shot be? Fruit and fizz make a delicious combination, and the glow you'll get will make you feel as if you're basking in the Malibu sunshine.

method

Don't pre-chill the ingredients, just pour the Malibu into the shot glass and add the cola.

Horny Bull

No.1: 1 part tequila • 1 part Southern Comfort
No.2: 1 part tequila • 1 part rum • 1 part vodka
No.3: 1 part tequila • 1 part light rum

There are a couple of variations: try them all out for size! The photograph shows a no. 1. Just keep away from red rags and you'll be fine.

method

Don't pre-chill the ingredients, simply pour the ingredients into the shot glass. Grab the bull by the horns and shoot!

Horny Mohican

1 part crème de banane • 1 part Baileys Irish Cream
1 part coconut rum

This drink has so much bite it will make your hair stand on end! Perfect for old-school punks and rockers. The creamy taste is very misleading: a few of these and you'll be pogo-ing till dawn.

method

Don't pre-chill the ingredients, just pour them into the shot glass.

Fancy a Horny Girl Scout? 1 part coffee liqueur and 1 part peppermint schnapps poured straight into a shot glass. Be prepared!

Jageritia

I part Jagermeister • I part tequila • I part lime juice

If you want something a little more ferocious than a cocktail, try this Margarita with attitude. You'll be dancing around your sombrero all night.

method

Don't chill the ingredients, just pour them straight into the shot glass.

Joe Cocker

1 part Amaretto • 1 part Southern Comfort
1 part Crown Royal bourbon • 1 part whiskey

Get by with a little help from this little friend. The original recipe called for Crown Royal bourbon, but Joe's a nice guy so he won't mind if you substitute!

method

Pour the ingredients straight – don't pre-chill into a shot glass. Now you know where Joe Cocker gets that magnificent scream!

Three Wise Men

1 part whisk(e)y • 1 part Jim Beam bourbon
1 part tequila

Wise men are like buses, you wait for ages, then three come along! We make no claim that this drink will make you any wiser, however.

method

Don't chill the ingredients, just pour straight into the shot glass.

How about Three Wise Men on a Farm? 1 part whisk(e)y; 1 part Jim Beam; 1 part Wild Turkey; 1 part Yukon Jack (a sweet, Canadian herb liqueur).

Meat & Potatoes

1 part vodka • 1 slice pepperoni

A fun shot for parties, and a lot quicker than preparing a Sunday roast! Make sure you use potato-based vodka, as meat and fruit doesn't have the same ring to it.

method

Chill the vodka – you can shake or stir with ice – and then strain into a shot glass. Garnish with the slice of pepperoni. It's a meal in a glass!

M & M

1 part Frangelico • 1 part white crème de cacao

Oooh, this one's for chocoholics everywhere. What could be more perfect than combining two vices at once: chocolate and alcohol? Pure decadence in a glass.

method

Don't chill the ingredients beforehand, just pour them straight into the shot glass.

Alien

1 part blue curacao • Splash of Baileys Irish Cream

The colour is like something from another planet, and the taste is out of this world. An alien invasion has never felt so good.

method

Chill the blue curacao – you can stir or shake it first with ice in the shaker to get it really cold – then strain into the shot glass. Slowly pour the Baileys into the centre and watch the alien life form appear.

Baby Guinness

1 part coffee liqueur (Tia Maria or Kahlua)
Splash of Baileys Irish Cream

It looks like a tiny glass of Guinness, it tastes like
nectar. Try mixing up a batch for a special party, and
you'll be singing Danny Boy like a good 'un.

method

*Pour the coffee liqueur into the shot glass. Now, very
slowly, pour the Baileys over the back (the rounded side)
of a spoon to float on top. If you prefer, you could use a
turkey baster to float the Baileys!*

Clear Layer Shot

*1 part lemon-lime soda • 1 part akvavit
1 part Grenadine*

A fun shot – with luck, the akvavit should settle in a layer at the top of the glass, but don't worry if it doesn't because the flavour combination is terrific however it works out.

method

Combine the akvavit and the lemon-lime soda in the glass. Slowly pour the Grenadine down the inside of the glass. It should settle into a layer at the bottom.

Cement Mixer

1 part Baileys Irish Cream • 1 part sweetened lime juice

Because Baileys Irish Cream (unlike crème liqueurs) does contain cream, mixing it with citrus juices will make it curdle. Most of the time in cocktails and mixed drinks this is avoided, but in shots, it makes for a very interesting experience!

method

Pour the Baileys into the shot glass and carefully pour the sweetened lime juice over the back (the rounded side) of a spoon so it floats on top. (If you want, you can use a turkey baster to add the lime juice!) The lime juice will cause the Baileys to curdle. Take the shot but roll it around in your mouth before swallowing!

Shaky Shots

These shots are made using a cocktail shaker. Simply put some ice cubes in the bottom of the shaker, pour in the ingredients, put the top on, and shake! The liquor is strained through the holes, leaving the ice behind. This makes the ingredients really chilled and thoroughly mixed together, but it does increase the volume of the drinks as you will be adding a little iced water each time. Make sure you measure accurately – use those graduated kitchen measuring spoons – and take account of the extra volume as you don't want to waste any of your precious shots!

Where a recipe includes a fizzy soda or mixer, I find it best to add this to the mix after shaking the other ingredients together and giving the whole mix a stir with a long-handled spoon or muddler. Shaking a fizzy ingredient in the shaker risks a foaming mass when you undo the cap – especially if you are making up a large batch of a recipe.

If you don't have a shaker, don't worry. You can always stir the ingredients really well together in a jug with ice cubes, then strain through a fine mesh sieve to keep the ice back.

Whatever method you use, have fun! And remember, as small as they are, these shots contain a lot of alcohol, so don't overdo them! Have plenty of water and fruit juices on hand for chasers.

Some of these shots were created using proprietary (branded) spirits and liqueurs and this is often reflected in their names. The original recipes are given, and while it's quite possible to substitute a proprietary spirit or liqueur with a generic version, bear in mind that any substitution will affect the final taste. Some of the recipes call for what is known as sweet and sour mix: you'll find the recipe for this on page 14.

Acapulco

1 part tequila • 1 part pineapple juice
1 part grapefruit juice

A touch of Mexican sunshine brought to you in a mix of tequila, pineapple and grapefruit juice.

method

Put some ice cubes into the shaker and pour in the juices. Add the tequila. Shake well and strain into a shot glass.

Absolut Quaalude

*1 part Absolut vodka • 1 part Frangelico
1 part Baileys Irish Cream*

An equally addictive alternative! Like the Hunter, also from the makers of Absolut Vodka, it makes use of coffee and hazelnut flavours.

method

Put some ice cubes into the shaker and pour in the ingredients. Shake well and strain into a shot glass.

Absolut Testa Rossa

2 parts Absolut vodka • 1 part Campari

Absolut vodka is here combined with Campari, the famous red-coloured Italian 'bitters', hence the 'Festa Rossa' (red head) name.

method

Place the ingredients in the shaker with some ice cubes. Shake and then strain into a shot glass.

Absolut Hunter

2 parts Absolut vodka • 1 part Jagermeister

This recipe comes courtesy of the makers of Absolut Vodka, which is mixed here with Jagermeister, a herby German 'bitters'.

method

Put some ice cubes in the shaker and pour in the Absolut vodka and Jagermeister. Shake and strain into a shot glass.

Advo Shot

2 parts blue curacao • 1 part Advocaat

Advocaat is a brandy-and-egg liqueur that is a speciality of Holland. Try this blue-orange mix!

method

Shake the ingredients with ice cubes in the shaker then strain into a shot glass.

American Apple Pie

I part cinnamon schnapps • I part apple juice

Apple pie with cinnamon in a glass! Cinnamon schnapps is just one of the numerous flavours available, and is terrific with apple juice.

method

Shake the ingredients with ice and then strain into a shot glass.

Coma

1 part dark rum • 1 part cinnamon schnapps

There are a few shots called Coma, testament to the effects of one too many! This version is an opportunity to use cinnamon schnapps.

method

Shake the ingredients with ice then strain into a shot glass.

After Dinner

1 part cognac (or brandy) • 1 part cherry brandy
Dash of lemon juice

Perfect for, well, after dinner! This is one shot you may prefer to 'sip' rather than 'shoot' – it tastes so good you won't want it to end!

method

Put the ingredients into a shaker along with some ice cubes. Shake and strain into a shot glass.

All Fall Down

1 part tequila • 1 part Kahlua • 1 part dark rum

That's what will happen after a couple of these shots! Rum and tequila are combined with coffee-flavoured Kahlua, a speciality of Mexico.

method

Put some ice cubes into a shaker and pour in the ingredients. Shake well and strain into a shot glass.

Alabama Slammer

No.1: 1 part Southern Comfort • 1 part Amaretto
Splash orange juice • Splash pineapple juice

No2: 2 parts Southern Comfort • 2 parts Amaretto
1 part sloe gin • Splash lemon juice

No3: 2 parts Southern Comfort • 1 part Amaretto
4 parts cranberry juice

There are a couple of variations on this theme – try them out for yourself. The photograph shows No. 1.

method

Put the ingredients into a shaker along with some ice cubes. Shake and strain into a shot glass.

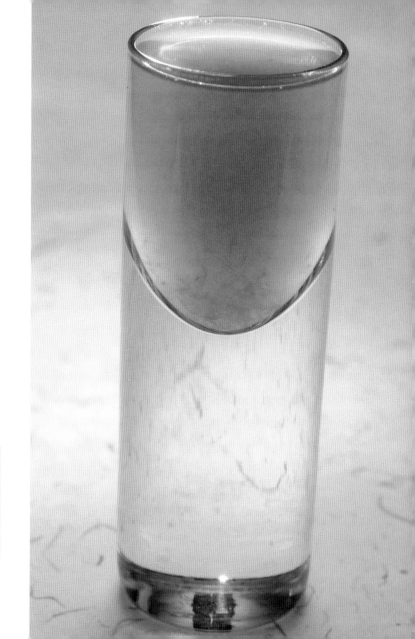

Alice from Dallas Shooter

1 part coffee liqueur (Tia Maria or Kahlua)
1 part Mandarine Napoleon • 1 part tequila gold

Beware those Texas gals! The smooth taste of this shot disguises a drink that packs a pretty powerful punch!

method

Put some ice cubes into a shaker and pour in the ingredients. Shake well and strain into a shot glass.

Agent Orange

1 part Southern Comfort • 1 part Jack Daniels
Splash orange juice

A glorious colour and a taste to match. This shot
makes use of two of America's finest products:
the delicate peach-flavoured Southern Comfort
and the famous Tennessee sour mash whiskey from
Jack Daniels.

method

Shake the ingredients with ice cubes then strain into a
shot glass.

Alternate

1 part crème de cassis • 1 part Midori
1 part pineapple juice

A pleasant change. Cassis is a crème liqueur made from blackcurrants, a speciality of Dijon in France, while Midori is the bright green, melon-flavoured liqueur from Japan.

method

Pour the ingredients into the shaker, along with some ice cubes. Shake and then strain into a shot glass.

Amalfi Drive

I part crème de banane • I part limoncello

Lemon trees line the streets of towns like Amalfi on the Bay of Naples in Italy. This shot uses limoncello, an intensely lemon-flavoured liqueur.

method

Put some ice cubes into a shaker and pour in the ingredients. Shake well and strain into a shot glass.

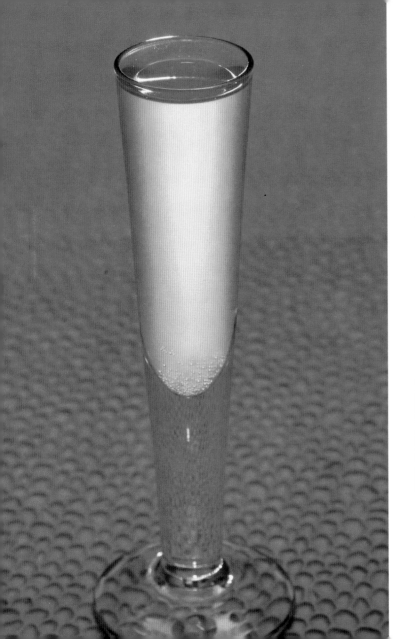

Amaretto Chill

1 part vodka • 1 part Amaretto
1 part pineapple juice • 1 part lemonade

A fruity-almond flavoured shot, based on vodka and
Amaretto, the deep amber-coloured, Italian liqueur.

method

*Put some ice cubes into the shaker and pour in the
pineapple juice, the vodka and the Amaretto. Shake well.
Take the lid off the shaker and pour in the lemonade.
Stir. Put the cap back on the shaker and strain the drink
into a shot glass.*

Amaretto Kamikaze

1 part vodka • 1 part Amaretto

Kamikaze means 'divine wind'. This shot is a breeze!
But beware: 2 or 3 could produce devastating
effects!

method

*Put some ice cubes into a shaker and pour in the
ingredients. Shake well and strain into a shot glass. For
an Amaretto Kumlhuzi, replace the vodka with tequila.*

Angels Rush Shooter

1 part Frangelico • 1 part cream

A creamy concoction with the flavour of hazelnuts.
Made for angels, but available to mortals too!

method

Put some ice cubes in the shaker and pour in the cream
and Frangelico. Shake well and strain into a shot glass.
Listen for the sound of angels' harps!

American Dream

Live the dream! This shot combines the flavour of nuts – almonds and hazelnuts – with chocolate and coffee.

method

Put the ingredients in the shaker along with some ice cubes and shake. Strain into a shot glass.

Angry Fijian

1 part crème de banane • 1 part Malibu

Can't imagine why anyone could be angry after this coconut banana delight!

method

Put some ice cubes into a shaker and pour in the ingredients. Shake well and strain into a shot glass.

Electric Kamikaze

*1 part vodka • 1 part Triple Sec/Cointreau
1 part blue curacao • 1 part lime juice*

Watch the sparks fly! The gorgeous colour in the shot is provided by the blue curacao, which has a distinct orange flavour.

method

Put the ingredients in the shaker along with some ice cubes and shake. Strain into a shot glass.

Antifreeze

I part vodka • I part green crème de menthe

Perfect for raising the temperature a few degrees!
The colour and the mint flavour come from the
green crème de menthe.

method

Put some ice cubes into a shaker and pour in the
ingredients. Shake well and strain into a shot glass.

Apricot Chill

2 parts apricot brandy • 1 part lemon juice
1 part pineapple juice

A fire and ice mix, courtesy of the apricot brandy.
Not a 'true' brandy, apricot brandy is made by
infusing the fruit in a spirit base.

method

Put some ice cubes into a shaker and pour in the
ingredients. Shake well and strain into a shot glass.

Bootlegger

*I part whisk(e)y • I part Southern Comfort
I part Sambuca*

Respect to all those prohibition-busters! Whiskey, peach-flavoured Southern Comfort and a hint of licquorice makes a very smooth shot.

method

Put some ice cubes into a shaker and pour in the ingredients. Shake well and strain into a shot glass.

B-54

1 part Baileys Irish Cream • 1 part Tia Maria or Kahlua coffee liqueur • 1 part green crème de menthe • 1 part Grand Marnier

Some say this has more fire power than a B-52! it's certainly an interesting combination of flavours.

method

Put the ingredients in the shaker along with some ice cubes and shake well. Strain into a shot glass.

Backstreet Romeo

1 part whiskey – preferably Irish!
1 part Baileys Irish Cream

Girls, this is the boy your mum warned you about!
The smoothness of the creamy Baileys hides the
knock-out effect of the whiskey!

method

*Put the ingredients in the shaker along with some ice
cubes and shake well. Strain into a shot glass.*

Ballistic Missile

Does what it says on the label. A cognac-based liqueur, Grand Marnier is the 'king' of the curacaos.

method

Put some ice cubes into a shaker and pour in the ingredients. Shake well and strain into a shot glass.

Bananarama

1 part vodka • 1 part crème de banane

Remember them? Remember the songs? If you can, you're old enough to be drinking this!

method

Put the ingredients in the shaker along with some ice cubes and shake. Strain into a shot glass.

Cactus Thorn

2 parts silver tequila • 1 part green crème de menthe
1 part freshly squeezed lime juice

Watch out, they're sharp! The 'cactus' refers to
the tequila, and the green colour comes from the
crème de menthe.

method

Put the ingredients in the shaker along with some ice
cubes and shake. Strain into a shot glass.

Black Forest Gateau

1 part cherry brandy • 1 part Tia Maria or Kahlua coffee liqueur • 1 part Baileys Irish Cream

Liquid cake! Cherry liqueur combined with a hint of coffee and lashings of cream.

method

Put the ingredients in the shaker along with some ice cubes and shake. Strain into a shot glass.

Blue Marlin

2 parts light rum • 1 part blue curacao
1 part lime juice

One big fish that didn't get away! The sweetness of the orange-flavoured blue curacao is tempered by the rum and lime juice.

method

Put the ingredients in the shaker along with some ice cubes and shake. Strain into a shot glass.

Avalanche

1 part Southern Comfort • 1 part coffee liqueur (Tia Maria or Kahlua) • 1 part dark crème de cacao

Starts slow, then builds in strength until it knocks you over!

method

Put some ice cubes into a shaker and pour in the ingredients. Shake well and strain into a shot glass.

Broken Down Golf Cart

1 part Amaretto • 1 part Midori • 1 part cranberry juice

Fortunately, it broke down on the 18th close to the clubhouse, where this remarkable mix gets things back on par.

method

Put some ice cubes into a shaker and pour in the ingredients. Shake well and strain into a shot glass.

Bat Bite

1 part Bacardi rum • 1 part cranberry juice

This drink comes from the bat logo of the world-famous Bacardi rum. Bats lived in the caves where the rum was aged!

method

Put some ice cubes into a shaker and pour in the ingredients. Shake well and strain into a shot glass.

California Surfer

1 part Malibu • 1 part Jagermeister
2 parts pineapple juice

Surfs up! A delicious combination of coconut
rum and Jagermeister!

method

Put the ingredients in the shaker along with some ice
cubes and shake. Strain into a shot glass.

Cream of Beef

1 part Baileys Irish Cream • 1 part Beefeater gin

The cream is Baileys, the beef is Beefeater gin,
of course!

Catfish

3 parts bourbon • 1 part peach schnapps

There's a sign on my door that says: Gone fishing!
There's a fair amount of bourbon in here and an
extra kick from the peach schnapps.

method

*Put some ice cubes into a shaker and pour in the
ingredients. Shake well and strain into a shot glass.*

Champerelle

1 part anisette • 1 part cognac • 1 part Cointreau

Ooh-la-la! France's finest produce in a neat little
shot with an aniseed flavour.

method

Put the ingredients in the shaker along with some ice
cubes and shake. Strain into a shot glass.

Choad

1 part green Chartreuse • 1 part tequila

Weird but wonderful! Green Chartreuse has been made since the 16th century by monks in France, while tequila was the tipple of the Aztec gods of Mexico.

method

Put the ingredients in the shaker along with some ice cubes and shake. Strain into a shot glass.

Comfort Special

2 parts Southern Comfort • I part sweet vermouth
I part orange juice

Just peachy! Southern Comfort was 'invented' by W. Heron in New Orleans in the 1880s. When he moved to St Louis he created the St Louis Cocktail, made with his secret-recipe peach-flavoured liqueur.

method

Put some ice cubes into a shaker and pour in the ingredients. Shake well and strain into a shot glass.

Calypso Cooler

1 part spiced rum • 1 part Amaretto
1 part orange juice • Dash of Grenadine

One for drinking aboard Jacques Cousteau's boat!
Spiced rum gives this shot an interesting 'bite':
try Captain Morgan's, one of the finest
proprietary brands.

method

*Pour the spiced rum, Amaretto and orange juice into the
shaker along with some ice cubes and shake. Strain into
a shot glass and top with the dash of Grenadine.*

shaky shots **105**

Cuervo Aztec Sky

1 part José Cuervo tequila • 1 part blue curacao

A tequila and blue curacao mix courtesy of José Cuervo tequila.

method

Put some ice cubes into a shaker and pour in the ingredients. Shake well and strain into a shot glass.

For a Cuervo Aztec Ruin replace the blue curacao with Roses Lime Juice.

Deckchair

1 part Southern Comfort • 1 part crème de banane
1 part orange juice

Relaxez-vous with this fruity delight – a delicious
mix of peach, banana and orange flavours.

method

Put some ice cubes into a shaker and pour in the
ingredients. Shake well and strain into a shot glass.

Death from Within

1 part light rum • 1 part dark rum • 1 part vodka

A potent little minx! Feel the heat rise up inside
after you've downed this shot!

method

*Put the ingredients in the shaker along with some ice
cubes and shake. Strain into a shot glass.*

Curtain Call

1 part Jagermeister • 1 part whisk(e)y • 1 part Midori

Bow out with this shot. It's so delicious, you may well have to come back for an encore!

method

Put the ingredients in the shaker along with some ice cubes and shake. Strain into a shot glass.

Unleaded

1 part dark rum • 1 part tequila gold

But still plenty of power in this high-octane mix of dark rum and golden tequila.

method

Put some ice cubes into a shaker and pour in the rum and tequila. Shake and strain into a shot glass.

Dirty Navel

1 part Triple Sec/Cointreau • 1 part white crème de cacao

You've had a fuzzy navel (page 112), now try a dirty one! This shot is a must for chocolate-lovers!

method

Put some ice cubes into a shaker and pour in the ingredients. Shake well and strain into a shot glass.

Fuzzy Navel

1 part vodka • 1 part peach schnapps
1 part orange juice

The fuzzy bits belong to peaches – peach schnapps
in this case!

method

Put the ingredients in the shaker along with some ice
cubes and shake. Strain into a shot glass.

Elvis Presley

1 part vodka • 1 part Frangelico
1 part Baileys Irish Cream • 1 part crème de banane

The King loved peanut butter and banana
sandwiches.

method

*Put the ingredients in the shaker along with some ice
cubes and shake. Strain into a shot glass.*

Fiery Blue Mustang

1 part Akvavit • 1 part crème de banane
1 part blue curacao

Go little pony! A gorgeous colour and an amazing
fruit flavour – with a kick!

method

*Put some ice cubes into a shaker and pour in the
ingredients. Shake well and strain into a shot glass.*

Fireball

1 part ouzo • 1 part coffee liqueur
(Tia Maria or Kahlua)

The flavours of an afternoon in a Greek cafe –
ouzo, the pastis of Greece, and coffee. A shot
that's worth lingering over a little longer!

method

Put the ouzo and the coffee liqueur in the shaker, along
with some ice cubes and shake. Strain into a shot glass.

Future Dance Squad

1 part sloe gin • 1 part dry vermouth

Start a new dance craze after a couple of these gloriously flavoured combinations of sloe gin and dry vermouth.

method

Put the sloe gin and vermouth into the shaker along with some ice cubes and shake. Strain into a shot glass.

Four Horsemen

1 part tequila • 1 part Sambuca • 1 part light rum
1 part Jagermeister

A devastating – but not Apocalyptical – combination of tequila, Sambuca, rum and Jagermeister. A flavour for each rider!

method

Pour the ingredients in the shaker along with some ice cubes and shake. Strain into a shot glass.

Freddy Kreuger

1 part Sambuca • 1 part Jagermeister • 1 part vodka

The villain of Nightmare on Elm Street. Now name the actor who played him!

method

Put some ice cubes into a shaker and pour in the Sambuca, vodka and Jagermeister. Shake well and strain into a shot glass.

Flat Tyre

2 parts tequila • 1 part Sambuca Negra

Probably bursts going over the cactus spines!
Mexico's finest (tequila) meets Italian Black Sambuca
with its very subtle hint of licquorice and coffee.

method

Put some ice cubes into a shaker and pour in the tequila
and Sambuca Negra. Shake well and strain into a shot
glass.

Green Demon

1 part vodka • 1 part light rum
1 part Midori (melon liqueur) • 1 part lemonade

A chance to use one of the most idiosyncratic liqueurs, the melon-flavoured Midori, which in Japanese means 'green'.

method

In a shaker with 2 or 3 ice cubes, shake the vodka, rum and Midori. Add the lemonade to the shaker. Do not shake but stir twice. Strain into a shot glass.

Gladiator

1 part Southern Comfort • 1 part Amaretto
1 part orange juice • 1 part lemon-lime soda

I'm Spartacus! A couple of these shots and you'll be ready to face combat.

method

Put some ice cubes into a shaker and pour in the Southern Comfort, Amaretto and orange juice. Shake well. Now add the lemon-lime soda and stir. Put the cap back on the shaker and strain the mix into a shot glass.

Uzi Shooter

1 part dry vermouth • 1 part Ricard (or Pernod)
1 part sugar syrup

Highly effective! A really sharp (-tasting) shooter that
hits the target every time!

method

Put some ice cubes into a shaker and pour in the
vermouth, Ricard and the sugar. Shake well and strain
into a shot glass.

Grasshopper Shot

1 part blue curacao • 3 parts cognac (or brandy)

An almost iridescent colour courtesy of the blue curacao, this shot also packs plenty of fire power.

method

Put the blue curacao and the cognac (or brandy) in the shaker along with some ice cubes and shake. Strain into a shot glass.

Greek Fire

1 part brandy (Metaxa if possible!) • 1 part ouzo

Greek fire was an incendiary mix of unknown ingredients used by the ancient Greeks to rain down on their enemies. While the ingredients in this shot are known quantities, it's still a pretty fiery mix!

method

Put the brandy and the ouzo in the shaker along with some ice cubes and shake. Strain into a shot glass.

Greek Revolution

1 part ouzo • 1 part Grenadine

Shout out 'Eloutheria!' (Freedom!) before shooting this gorgeous aniseed-and-fruit-flavoured shot!

method

Put some ice cubes into a shaker and pour in the ouzo and the Grenadine. Shake and strain into a shot glass.

Gumball Shooter

1 part Sambuca • 1 part blue curacao

An aniseed-and-citrus-flavoured shot that's really
deceptive! It tastes harmless, but beware the
aftershock!

method

Put some ice cubes into a shaker and pour in the
Sambuca and blue curacao. Shake and strain into a shot
glass.

Ghostbuster

I part vodka • I part Midori • I part pineapple juice
I part orange juice

Who you gonna call? A wonderfully weird colour
courtesy of the melon-flavoured Midori.

method

Put some ice cubes into a shaker and pour in the ingredients. Shake well and strain into a shot glass.

Galactic Ale

1 part vodka • 1 part blue curacao • 1 part lime juice
1 part crème de framboise (raspberry liqueur)

For space cadets everywhere, a chance to explore
new flavours and to seek out new liqueurs.

method

*In a shaker with 2 or 3 ice cubes, shake all the
ingredients vigorously. Then strain into a shot glass.*

Harley Davidson

I part Jägermeister • I part Midori
I part Baileys Irish Cream

Hog heaven in a glass! This is a truly inspired
combination of flavours. Go on, take the ride
of your life!

method

Put the ingredients in the shaker along with some ice
cubes and shake. Strain into a shot glass.

Peppermint Pattie

1 part white crème de menthe • 1 part white crème de cacao

Very simple to make, but a wonderful subtle chocolate-mint flavour.

method

Place the ingredients in a shaker with some ice cubes. Shake and strain into a shot glass.

Hazelnut Chill

1 part Frangelico • 1 part pineapple juice
1 part lemonade

Nutty! Frangelico is an Italian liqueur made from
wild hazelnuts. It comes in a terrific bottle – shaped
like a monk, complete with rope belt!

method

Put some ice cubes into a shaker and pour in the
Frangelico and pineapple juice. Shake well, then add the
lemonade and stir a couple of times. Strain into a shot
glass.

Oh My Gosh

1 measure peach schnapps • 1 measure Amaretto

This is a wonderful winter-time warmer, especially if you've just come in from the cold.

method

Add 2 or 3 ice cubes to the shaker. Pour in the peach schnapps and Amaretto and shake. Strain into a shot glass.

Hay Fever Remedy

1 part vodka • 1 part Southern Comfort
1 part Amaretto • 1 part pineapple juice
Dash of Grenadine

It might not actually cure your hayfever, but it will certainly take your mind off it! Feel better almost instantly, then undo all the good by having a second shot!

method

Shake all the ingredients with 2 or 3 ice cubes in a shaker. Strain into a shot glass.

Sex Under the Moonlight

I part vodka • I part coffee liqueur
(Tia Maria or Kahlua) • I part port • Splash of cream

For the truly romantic! A curious combination of
ingredients, but an amazing flavour.

method

Put some ice cubes into a shaker and pour in the
ingredients. Shake and strain into a shot glass.

Sex on the Beach

1 part vodka • 1 part peach schnapps
1 part cranberry juice • 1 part orange juice

Go on, ask the bartender for this! One of the most famous shots, it has a terrific fruity flavour that can be quite addictive!

method

Put the ingredients in the shaker along with some ice cubes and shake. Strain into a shot glass.

Scorpion Suicide

1 part cherry brandy • 1 part whisk(e)y
1 part Pernod

A real stinger! The famous French pastis, Pernod,
gives this shot a slightly 'milky' appearance.

method

Put some ice cubes into a shaker and pour in the
ingredients. Shake and strain into a shot glass.

Silver Bullet

1 part gin • 1 part Scotch • Lemon twist

Werewolves beware. Being shot with a silver bullet is the end!

method

Put some ice cubes into a shaker and pour in the gin and Scotch. Shake and strain into a shot glass and garnish with the lemon twist

Teen Wolf

1 part Advocaat • 1 part cherry brandy

Such difficult years! An inspired recipe that makes terrific use of the Dutch brandy and egg-based Advocaat.

method

Put some ice cubes into a shaker and pour in the Advocaat and cherry brandy. Shake and strain into a shot glass.

Golden Russian

1 part vodka • 1 part Galliano

A tasty mix of vodka and Galliano, a vanilla-and-herb-flavoured liqueur named after an Italian general.

method

Put some ice cubes into a shaker and pour in the vodka and Galliano. Shake well and strain into a shot glass.

Waterloo Shooter

1 part Mandarine Napoleon • 1 part spiced rum
1 part orange juice

For when you put Abba records on! Waterloo, the site of the battle between the French and the English, is in Belgium, the home of Mandarine Napoleon.

method

Put the ingredients in the shaker along with some ice cubes and shake. Strain into a shot glass.

Squished Smurf

1 part peach schnapps • 1 part Baileys Irish Cream
1 part blue curacao • Dash of Grenadine

Remember those annoying creatures? Well, they're squished now. A 'strange'-coloured shot, but a fantastic taste.

method

Put some ice cubes into a shaker and pour in the ingredients. Shake and strain into a shot glass.

Red Beard

1 part Captain Morgan spiced rum • 1 Malibu
Splash of Grenadine • Splash of lemon-lime soda

For pirates everywhere! A perfect blend of spiced
and coconut rums with a hint of tropical fruit.

method

Put the ingredients (except the lemon-lime soda) in the
shaker, along with some ice cubes and shake. Strain into
a shot glass and top with the lemon-lime soda.

Rick

1 part Sambuca • 1 part orange juice

Of all the bars... I doubt that Bogart served these in his *Casablanca* bar – maybe if he had, Bergman would have never got on that plane!

method

Put some ice cubes into a shaker and pour in the Sambuca and orange juice. Shake and strain into a shot glass.

Redneck Marine

1 part Jagermeister • 1 part whiskey • 1 part akvavit

Your country needs you! A great opportunity to crack open the Akvavit.

method

Put some ice cubes into a shaker and pour in the Jagermeister, whiskey and akvavit. Shake and strain into a shot glass.

Turkey Shoot

1 part Wild Turkey • 1 part anisette

Shoot that bird! Wild Turkey straight Kentucky bourbon is available as both 43% abv and 50.5% abv, known as Wild Turkey 101. Choose your weapon!

method

Put the ingredients in the shaker along with some ice cubes and shake. Strain into a shot glass.

Pineapple Bomb

1 part Southern Comfort • 1 part Triple Sec or Cointreau
1 part pineapple juice

Surely that's a hand grenade? The peach flavour of the Southern Comfort and the orange of the Triple Sec are complemented by pineapple juice.

method

Put the ingredients in the shaker along with some ice cubes and shake. Strain into a shot glass.

Purple Rain

1 part vodka • 1 part blue curacao
Splash cranberry juice

Homage to the 'artist formerly known as Prince',
who would have loved this gorgeous-tasting and
coloured shot.

method

*Put some ice cubes into a shaker and pour in the vodka,
curacao and cranberry juice. Shake and strain into a
shot glass.*

shaky shots **147**

Poison Apple

1 part Calvados or applejack • 1 part vodka

Only Snow White should beware this fruity treat. The vodka is the 'poison' (vodka is a neutral spirit that is essentially 'flavourless') and the apple comes from Calvados or Applejack – apple brandies.

method

Put some ice cubes into a shaker and pour in the vodka and the Calvados/applejack. Shake and strain into a shot glass.

Porto Covo

1 part vodka • 1 part absinthe (or Pernod)
1 part Malibu • 1 part crème de banane

Sounds like a nice place! Absinthe is a remarkably potent spirit – it was known by artists in the 19th century as 'the green fairy'. Too many of these and you'll see them too!

method

Put the vodka, absinthe, crème de banane and Malibu in the shaker along with some ice cubes and shake. Strain into a shot glass.

Rabbit Punch

1 part Campari • 1 part dark crème de cacao
1 part Baileys Irish Cream • 1 part Malibu

Specially designed for mad March hares: say 'white rabbit, white rabbit' as you raise your shot. Take a second shot and see if you can still pronounce the 'r' in rabbit!

method

Put the ingredients in the shaker along with some ice cubes and shake. Strain into a shot glass.

Paddy's Day Special

1 part green crème de menthe • 1 part Triple Sec or Cointreau • 1 part Midori

Celebrate St Patricks day with this one! A suitably green-coloured shot, but the flavours are far removed from the 'Emerald Isle'.

method

Put the ingredients in the shaker along with some ice cubes and shake. Strain into a shot glass.

Purple Hooter

1 part vodka (try a citrus vodka if you want!)
1 part Triple Sec or Cointreau • Dash of crème de
framboise (raspberry liqueur)

A gorgeous colour and a great taste, too. A distinctly
fruity shot – full of oranges and raspberries!

method

Shake the ingredients with 2 or 3 ice cubes in a shaker
and strain into a shot glass.

Pistol Shot

1 part Triple Sec or Cointreau • 1 part cherry brandy
1 part apricot brandy

Goes down great guns. A sweet-tasting shot packed with fruit flavours.

method

Put the ingredients in the shaker along with some ice cubes and shake. Strain into a shot glass.

Woo-Woo Shooter

1 part vodka • 1 part peach schnapps
1 part cranberry juice

Once known as the Teeny-Weeny Woo-Woo, the original Woo-Woo came to fame in the 1980s as a highball (long) drink. Here it is as a shooter: prepared to be wooed and wowed!

method

Shake with 2 or 3 ice cubes in a shaker then strain into a shot glass.

Paralyser

1 part Tia Maria or Kahlua • 1 part vodka
1 part cola • 1 part milk

You might only need two to get a result. Yes, it contains milk and cola – but don't overlook the vodka and coffee liqueur!

method

Put some ice cubes into a shaker and pour in the coffee liqueur, the vodka and the milk. Shake, pour in the cola and stir, then strain into a shot glass.

Ponderosa

1 part akvavit • 1 part orangeade

Bonanza! A very simple, but highly effective, shot. Why not try Norwegian akvavit? Lysholm Linie akvavit has crossed the equator twice by ship!

method

Chill the akvavit by shaking it with some ice. Pour the orangeade into the shaker and stir. Strain into a shot glass.

Trick Shots
Fancy, Coloured, Layered
Shots for Steady Hands!

Bartenders call these drinks pousse-cafés – 'after coffee'. In the last 20 years or so, pousse-cafés have enjoyed something of a renaissance, in the form of shooters.

A pousse-café is a series of liqueurs and spirits (and other ingredients such as cream!) floating on top of each other in the glass in a sort of quaffable rainbow! In this section you'll find some easy ones – with two layers – along with some three-layered drinks. The trick is that different liqueurs have different weights, and this means they have to be poured in ascending order of lightness. Often, the level at the top is a spirit.

The technique requires a steady hand: each liqueur needs to be poured very slowly over the back (the rounded side) of a spoon. It helps to decant the liqueurs into small jugs, as this makes it a lot easier to control the flow of alcohol than from a full-sized bottle. You can cheat, though, and use a turkey baster! Gently dribble the liqueur over the spoon, drop by drop to form a layer. It's also a lot easier to create neat divisions between the different levels if you select glasses with straight sides: pousse-café glasses are by nature tall and narrow, a bit like tubes!

Don't worry if you end up with a drink that's a little wobbly – it happens! The beauty of these shot recipes is that if the layering goes wrong, you can shake or stir the drink, drink it straight up or on the rocks. So have fun!

Beam Me Up Scotty

1 part Kahlua • 1 crème de banane
1 part Baileys Irish Cream

Be transported! Bananas and cream with a hint of coffee in a glowing tower of tastes.

method

Layer the ingredients in the glass in the order shown by pouring each of the ingredients slowly over the back of a spoon. Alternatively, shake with ice and strain into the glass.

Advosary

1 part Advocaat • 2 parts maraschino

Legend says that the Dutch invented Advocaat after travellers in the East Indies discovered a native drink made out of the pulp of avocado pears. Others maintain that the brandy-and-egg liqueur acquired its name for its ability to loosen the tongue and enable even the most quiet to speak like an advocate (lawyer)!

method

Layer the ingredients in the glass in the order shown. Alternatively, you can shake with ice then strain into a glass.

After Eight

1 part white crème de menthe • 1 part coffee liqueur (Tia Maria or Kahlua) • 1 part Baileys Irish Cream

Coffee and mints are the traditional post-prandial offerings. Here they are, all in a glass!

method

Layer the ingredients in the glass in the order shown by pouring each of the ingredients slowly over the back of a spoon. Alternatively, shake with ice and strain into the glass.

After Nine

1 part Kahlua • 1 part peach schnapps
1 part Baileys Irish Cream

Still peckish? Try this tasty layer-cake of coffee,
peaches and cream.

method

Layer the ingredients in the glass in the order shown by
pouring each of the ingredients slowly over the back of a
spoon.

B-52

(classic) 1 part Kahlua • 1 part Baileys Irish Cream
1 part Grand Marnier

(variation) 1 part Kahlua • 1 part Baileys
1 part Cointreau

This drink is pretty famous, although many recipe books give different quantities for the ingredients, and even different ingredients depending on the author's particular preference for a liqueur! We'll keep it simple and use equal measures.

method

Pour each of the ingredients slowly over the back of a spoon into the glass in the order shown. Alternatively, shake with ice and strain into the glass.

For a B-53: 1 part Kahlua, 1 part Sambuca, 1 part Grand Marnier. Layer in the glass in the order shown.

Blow Job

No 1 1 part coffee liqueur • 1 part Amaretto • Whipped cream
No 2 1 part coffee liqueur • 1 part Baileys Irish cream • Whipped cream
No 3 1 part coffee liqueur • 1 part vodka • Whipped cream
No 4 1 part Baileys Irish Cream • 1 part crème de banane • Whipped cream
No 5 1 part Baileys Irish Cream • 1 part Grand Marnier • Whipped cream

No self-respecting shooter book would be complete without this! In fact, there are several variations on this theme. Some bars insist you also drink these without using your hands! We've shown No. 3 here.

method

Pour each of the ingredients slowly over the back of a spoon into the glass in the order shown and finally float the whipped cream on top. Alternatively, stir the ingredients together with ice, strain and then float the cream on top.

Book Me An Ambulance

I part yellow Chartreuse • I part cherry brandy
I part absinthe

This shooter contains some pretty strong stuff, so
you may just need that ride after all!

method

*Pour each of the ingredients slowly over the back of a
spoon into the glass in the order shown.*

For My Next Trick

1 part Grenadine • 1 part dark crème de cacao
1 part green crème de menthe • 1 part blue curacao
1 part maraschino • 1 part green Chartreuse

Once you've got the hang of layering drinks you can have fun with the ingredients and colours and make a rainbow! Try this six shooter for fun!

method

Starting with the Grenadine, gently pour each of the ingredients over the back of a spoon into the glass in the order given.

Chocolate Almond

1 part dark crème de cacao • 1 part Amaretto
1 part Baileys Irish Cream

Better than chewing, no nutty bits stuck in your
teeth!

method

*Layer the ingredients into a glass by pouring them in the
order shown over the back of a spoon.*

Blue Eyed Blonde

1 part crème de banane • 1 part blue curacao
1 part Baileys Irish Cream

It (almost) looks like one! This bombshell's eyes are
blue curacao, but if you prefer your blondes with
green eyes, try Midori instead!

method

Pour each of the ingredients slowly over the back of a
spoon into the glass in the order shown.

Caramilk

2 parts white crème de cacao
1 part crème de banane • 1 part Tia Maria or Kahlua

A sweet mix of chocolate, banana and coffee
flavours. In a word: lunch.

method

Layer the ingredients into a glass by pouring them gently
in the order given over the back of a spoon. If it all goes
wrong, just stir it together, it's still yummy!

Blue Thrill

1 part lemon juice • 1 part blue curacao

A good pousse-café to start off with, and a nice
fruity taste too.

method

Float the blue curacao on top of the lemon juice.

The Devil You Don't Know

1 part dark crème de cacao • 1 part Jagermeister

Ever wondered what you were missing when you opted for the Devil You Know? Now is your chance to find out in this chocolate-flavoured shot!

method

Pour each of the ingredients slowly over the back of a spoon into the glass in the order shown.

Coconut
Cream Pie

1 part chilled Malibu • Whipped cream

A real easy one! If you can't manage this, stick to shaken shots! If you've a sweet tooth, this shot will be ideal for you.

method

Chill the Malibu – either stir or shake with some ice – then strain into the glass. Float the whipped cream on top.

trick shots **171**

Cross-cultural Black Russian

I part Kahlua • I part Tia Maria • I part vodka

The original Black Russian was a mix of vodka and either Kahlua or Tia Maria. This Cross-cultural version shows the eclectic mix of contemporary culture. Either that, or we're just being greedy!

method

Pour each of the ingredients slowly over the back of a spoon into the glass in the order shown. Alternatively, shake with ice and strain into the glass.

City Hot Shot

1 part Grenadine • 1 part blue curacao
1 part Triple Sec

For when the markets close and the deals have
been done, try this colourful citrus shot.

method

*Layer the ingredients into a glass by pouring them gently
in the order given over the back of a spoon.*

Green Fly Shooter

1 part Midori • 1 part green crème de menthe

It's small, green and can wreak havoc among tender shoot(er)s! This is an inspired flavour combination – melon and mint – and a gorgeous colour, too!

method

Pour each of the ingredients slowly over the back of a spoon into the glass in the order shown. Alternatively, shake with ice and strain into the glass.

Electric Banana

1 part crème de banane • 1 part tequila

It's a banana with a mains voltage. The first flavour
to hit your tongue is tequila, followed swiftly
by banana.

method

*Pour the crème de banane into the glass, then gently
pour in the tequila so it floats on top.*

Elphino

1 part Sambuca • 1 part Triple Sec

A very simple yet delicious aniseed-citrus combination. You can use golden Sambuca or Negra (black) for dramatic effect.

method

Pour the Sambuca into the glass and gently float the Triple Sec on top.

The Girl Mum Warned You About

1 part Grenadine • 1 part Midori • 1 part blue curacao
1 part Triple Sec/Cointreau • 1 part rum

She can be tricky, and she may let you down, but
she's worth trying for!

method

Pour the ingredients gently over the back of a spoon in
the order shown.

Doucet Devil

1 part crème de banane • 2 parts Amaretto
1 part Southern Comfort

Not quite so devilish! Very softly coloured layers of golden liqueurs, but three very distinct flavours.

method

Pour each of the ingredients slowly over the back of a spoon into the glass in the order shown.

Necrophiliac

1 part Advocaat • 1 part blue curacao

A strange pastime for strange people. This is a really tasty shot: citrus at the top and creamy brandy at the base.

method

Pour the Advocaat into the glass, and then float the blue curacao on the top.

Hot to Trot

1 part cinnamon schnapps • Dash of lime juice
1 part tequila

This is a terrific spicy shot, if you dare! The dash of lime juice between the two 'hard' layers really kicks your tastebuds!

method

Pour the schnapps into the glass and layer the dash of lime juice on top. Gently float the tequila on top and shoot.

Tequila Mockingbird

1 part Amaretto • 1 part tequila

Great pun, great shooter! The taste of tequila combines perfectly with the almond-flavoured Amaretto.

method

Layer in a shot glass.

White Lightning

I part tequila • I part white crème de cacao

Tequila and chocolate, the food and drink of the Aztec gods. Tequila was 'discovered' by the Aztecs after their gods sent a lightning-bolt from heaven which landed on an agave plant and 'cooked' it into the spirit's drink!

method

Pour the tequila in the shot glass and float the white crème de cacao on top.

B.B.C.

1 part Baileys Irish Cream • *1 part Benedictine*
1 part Cointreau

Not, in fact, named after the British Broadcasting Corporation, but a handy mnemonic for the ingredients.

method

Layer the ingredients in the glass, pouring them into the glass in the order given. For a B.B.G. substitute Grand Marnier for the Cointreau.

Battered, Bruised & Bleeding

1 part Grenadine • 1 part blue curacao
1 part Midori

The battered part is the blue curacao, the bruised is the green Midori, and the bleeding the red of the Grenadine. The only thing that is assaulted, though, is your tongue!

method

Layer the ingredients in the glass, pouring them into the glass in the order given.

Red Hot

Dash of hot sauce • 1 part tequila
1 part cinnamon schnapps

A real hot shot! If you're really daring, substitute a
dash of wasabi for the hot sauce!

method

Put the hot sauce into the bottom of the shot glass. Next
pour in the tequila, then layer the cinnamon schnapps
on top.

E.T.

1 part Midori • 1 part Baileys Irish Cream
1 part vodka

Phone home and say you'll be late! In most layered shots, Baileys makes the topmost layer and forms a creamy head. Try it here sandwiched between Midori and vodka.

method

Layer the ingredients in the shot glass by pouring them in the order given slowly over the back of a spoon.

Late Bloomer

I part apricot brandy • I part Triple Sec • I part rum

Better late than never! A very tasty combination
of rum, oranges and apricots in subtly
coloured layers.

method

*Pour the apricot brandy into the glass, then layer on the
Triple Sec and float the rum on top.*

Fisherman's Wharf

I part Amaretto • I part Triple Sec
I part Courvoisier/cognac

A great shot for when you're sitting on a dock by the bay. This original recipe uses Courvoisier cognac.

method

Layer the ingredients in the glass in the order given above.

188 trick shots

Stormy Weather

1 part Sambuca Negra • 1 part whipped cream

The white whipped cream floating on black Sambuca makes this shot look like thunder clouds in a glass! It's a fun shot and a great alternative to 'after-dinner' coffee.

method

Pour the Sambuca Negra into the glass to create the dark sky. Float the whipped cream on top to make clouds!

Streetcar

1 part dark crème de cacao • 1 part Baileys Irish Cream
1 part apricot brandy

A streetcar that should be named Desire. This shot contains the flavours of chocolate, coffee, cream and apricots with whiskey and brandy undertones.

method

Layer the ingredients in the order shown in the shot glass.

Redback Shooter

I part Advocaat • I part Sambuca

An interesting combination. You can use black or golden Sambuca – and why not try some flavoured Advocaats too? Mocha and chocolate are available!

method

Pour the Advocaat into the glass and then gently pour in the Sambuca so that it floats on top.

Lovelorn

1 part apricot brandy • 1 part dry vermouth

Shoot yourself on February 15th! And live to fight another day. A very simple shot, yet very effective at mending broken hearts.

method

Float the dry vermouth on top of the apricot brandy.

P.H.

1 part Amaretto • 1 part pineapple juice
1 part Southern Comfort • Dash of lime juice

Perfectly balanced: not too sweet not too sour!
A fruit-and-nut-flavoured shot that looks a little
like a bumble bee.

method

Layer the ingredients in the shot glass by pouring them
in the order given slowly over the back of a spoon.

Liquid Asphalt

I part Sambuca • I part Jagermeister

For a realistic approach, try using Sambuca Negra (black Sambuca) to make the asphalt!

method

Float the Jagermeister on top of the Sambuca and shoot.

Dagger

1 part white crème de cacao • 1 part peach schnapps
1 part tequila

Is this a dagger I see before me? Lady Macbeth had
obviously had one too many!

method

Layer the ingredients in the shot glass by pouring them
in the order given slowly over the back of a spoon.

trick shots **195**

Pipeline

1 part vodka • 1 part tequila

Clears blocked pipes for certain! This is a great shot
if you've got unsteady hands – the two layers are
almost imperceptible – except on the tongue!

method

Layer in a shot glass and shoot!

Reality Twist

1 part blue curacao • 1 part Amaretto

Enter a different dimension with a couple of
shots of this! The 'blue sky' lies underneath the
'dark Earth' in this upside-down world!

method

*Pour the blue curacao into the shot glass and gently float
the Amaretto on top.*

Six Shooters
Party Shots and Jellies

No matter what you are celebrating, serving drinks is one of the best ways of getting the party going. Be warned, though, that while alcohol certainly makes for fun, it can also bring out the worst in people, including the hosts!

Party shots are a great way of keeping the party on track: three or four shots per person are plenty, and if they are interspersed with conversation, food and party games and quizzes, the emphasis is on a good time, rather than just drinking.

In this section, you'll find recipes for party shots and shooters, because they contain a fair number of ingredients and are actually easier to make in volume than as individual drinks. In general, the recipes will make around six shots, which is why I've called them Six Shooters! Just shake them and pour them into shot glasses and hand them around. Mixing shots in this way means that, as host, you can keep tabs on the number of shots guests have had. Remember, each shot glass holds around 5.7 cl/ 2 fl oz and around half of the shot, if not a little more, will be made up of spirits and liqueurs with pretty high levels of alcohol by volume! You can use a bar jigger or a shot glass as a measure, but don't forget that because you'll be shaking the ingredients with ice you'll be increasing the volume of the final mix. It's a good idea to practise first using plain water to check the measure, that way you won't waste any of the precious spirits and liqueurs!

Alongside the Six Shooter recipes, you'll also find recipes for some types of shooters that have recently become really popular in bars and at parties: these are gelatine shots, variously called jelly shots, Jell-o shots (after the proprietary brand of North American fruit-flavoured gelatine) and jiggelos.

While contemporary gelatine shots started their lives in the 1980s as novelty drinks favoured by college students, the origins of flavouring gelatine with alcohol go back to the early years of the 20th century. In the United States, one Otis Glidden produced a gelatine product that included a small glass vial of flavouring suspended in alcohol. This, the first gelatine shooter, was on sale for just a few years, until prohibition was introduced! In recent years, and riding on the crest of the wave of interest in classic cocktails, creative bartenders across the world have transformed the gelatine shot into a rather trendy cocktail.

You don't drink gelatine shots, you eat them. You can do this with a spoon, or you can squeeze them out of the little disposable cups, slurping and sucking them into your mouth! Disposable plastic shot glasses and jiggelo cups are now widely available. They are sometimes called soufflé cups and you can get them at most good retailers or buy on-line. For the ultimate in luxury, you could even create a gelatine shot in an edible chocolate cup. Look in the home-baking section in supermarkets for these! If you don't have any containers, you can always set them in ice cube trays and rubber moulds, or even in baking pans/trays and then cut them into mouth-sized cubes! You'll find more information about gelatine shots, such as using unflavoured gelatine and vegetarian gelatine, on pages 14-15.

Sexy Alligator

1 measure Malibu • 1 measure Midori
1 measure Jagermeister • 1 measure crème de framboise
(raspberry liqueur) • 1 measure pineapple juice

Tropical, green and a big bite! This is a really terrific combination of flavours: coconut, melon, raspberries, pineapple and herbs.

method

Put some ice cubes into the shaker. Using a jigger or shot glass, measure out equal amounts of the ingredients and pour them into the shaker. Shake and then strain into 6 shot glasses. If, for some strange reason you'd rather have Sex with an Alligator, simply omit the Malibu!

Chevy

1 measure Southern Comfort • 1 measure Triple Sec
1 measure Amaretto • ½ measure orange juice
½ measure pineapple juice • ½ measure Grenadine
½ measure lemon-lime soda

Cruise in a classic, but dont drink and drive! This fruit-flavoured shot is more powerful than you think!

method

Put some ice cubes into the shaker. Using a jigger or shot glass, measure out equal amounts of the ingredients, except for the lemon-lime soda, and pour them into the shaker. Shake, pour in the lemon-lime soda and stir, and then strain into 6 shot glasses.

Unholy Water

I measure gin • I measure akvavit
I measure spiced rum • I measure tequila
I measure vodka

But a heavenly taste! There are no fruit juices or mixers in this drink, just plain old alcohol, so watch how many you shoot, or things might just get a little hellish!

method

Put some ice cubes into the shaker. Using a jigger or shot glass, measure out equal amounts of the ingredients and pour them into the shaker. Shake and then strain into 6 shot glasses.

Pink Belly

1 measure Jim Beam bourbon • 1 measure Amaretto
1 measure sloe gin • 1 measure Baileys Irish Cream
1 measure lemon-lime soda

After a couple of shots of this, you'll find some folks
can't help showing you theirs!

method

*Put some ice cubes into the shaker. Using a jigger or shot
glass, carefully measure out equal amounts of the
ingredients, except for the lemon-lime soda, and pour
them into the shaker. Shake, pour in the lemon-lime soda
and stir, and then strain into 6 shot glasses.*

Illusion

1 measure Malibu • 1 measure Midori
1 measure vodka • 1 measure Cointreau
½ measure pineapple juice

It's magic! This pale green delight gets its colour from
Midori and its slightly coconut flavour from Malibu.

method

Put some ice cubes into the shaker. Using a jigger or shot
glass, carefully measure out equal amounts of the
ingredients and pour them into the shaker. Shake well
and then strain into 6 shot glasses.

Memory Loss

1 measure crème de banane • 1 measure vodka
1 measure crème de framboise (raspberry liqueur)
1 measure cranberry juice • 1 measure orange juice

Blame this if you can't remember what you did last night! Be warned, its fruity flavour may make you forget it's alcohol.

method

Put some ice cubes into the shaker. Using a jigger or shot glass, carefully measure out equal amounts of the ingredients and pour them into the shaker. Shake well and then strain into 6 shot glasses.

Liquid Cocaine

No. 1 1 measure tequila • 1 measure vodka • 1 measure gin
1 measure light rum • 1 measure akvavit • 1 measure lemon-lime soda
No. 2 1 measure vodka • 1 measure Amaretto • 1 measure Southern
Comfort • 1 measure Cointreau • 1 measure pineapple juice

A number of recipes go by this name – just goes to
show, you can never tell what's really in them. And
all of it hard stuff! The one in the picture is the No.1.

method

*No 1: Put some ice cubes into the shaker. Using a jigger
or shot glass, carefully measure out equal amounts of
the ingredients, except for the lemon-lime soda, and pour
them into the shaker. Shake, pour in the lemon-lime soda
and stir, and then strain into 6 shot glasses.*

*No 2: Put some ice cubes into the shaker. Using a jigger
or shot glass, carefully measure out equal amounts of
the ingredients and pour them into the shaker. Shake
well and then strain into 6 shot glasses.*

Lava Lamp

1 measure Tia Maria or Kahlua
1 measure crème de fraise (strawberry liqueur)
1 measure Frangelico • 6 drops of Advocaat

Remember those mesmerising, swirling blobs of colour floating in a glass lantern? Well, they're back!

method

Put some ice cubes into the shaker and using the jigger or shot glass, carefully measure out the ingredients and pour them all, except for the Advocaat, into the shaker. Shake and strain into 6 shot glass. Now put a single drop of Advocaat into the centre of each shot and make mini lava lamps!

Laser Beam

2 measures Southern Comfort • 2 measures Midori
1 measure Amaretto • 1 measure Triple Sec
2 measures pineapple juice

Very sci-fi! Perfect for mad scientists, and a terrific 'neon' colour.

method

Put some ice cubes into the shaker. Using a jigger or shot glass, carefully measure out equal amounts of the ingredients and pour them into the shaker. Shake well and then strain into 6 shot glasses.

Pants on Fire

1 measure vodka • 1 measure crème de fraise
(strawberry liqueur) • 1 measure crème de banane
1 measure orange juice

Best drunk during a game of Truth or Dare, at
least you can then shout the old playground taunt:
'liar, liar, pants on fire'. Or did I go to a particularly
rough school?

method

Put some ice cubes into the shaker. Using a jigger or shot
glass, carefully measure out equal amounts of the
ingredients and pour them into the shaker. Shake well
and then strain into 6 shot glasses.

G.T.O.

1 measure rum • 1 measure gin • 1 measure vodka
1 measure Southern Comfort • 1 measure Amaretto
1 measure Grenadine • 1 measure orange juice

A supercharged shooter. The gorgeous colour is created by the Grenadine, a pink syrup made from pomegranates.

method

Put some ice cubes into the shaker. Using a jigger or shot glass, carefully measure out equal amounts of the ingredients and pour them into the shaker. Shake and then strain into 6 shot glasses. Mirror, signal, manoeuvre.

Gross One

1 measure vodka • 1 measure Sambuca
1 measure whisk(e)y • 1 measure gin
1 measure Amaretto

How you might feel and be described as in the morning! Look at those ingredients: five measures of alcohol and not a drop of mixer. Be warned!

method

Put some ice cubes into the shaker. Using a jigger or shot glass, carefully measure out equal amounts of the ingredients and pour them into the shaker. Shake and then strain into 6 shot glasses. On your own heads be it!

Johnny on the Beach

I measure vodka • I measure Midori
I measure crème de cassis • I measure pineapple juice
I measure orange juice • I measure grapefruit juice
I measure cranberry juice

This is a classic among shots and everyone has their own version of the origin of the name. But everyone agrees that it tastes fantastic!

method

Put some ice cubes into the shaker. Using a jigger or shot glass, carefully measure out equal amounts of the ingredients and pour them into the shaker. Shake and then strain into 6 shot glasses.

212

Grapevine

1 measure cognac or brandy
1 measure apricot brandy • 1 measure crème de banane
1 measure maraschino • 1 measure Triple Sec

You heard it through the grapevine. The name refers to the various 'brandies' in here, but only cognac is a true grape brandy.

method

Put some ice cubes into the shaker. Using a jigger or shot glass, carefully measure out equal amounts of the ingredients and pour them into the shaker. Shake and then strain into 6 shot glasses.

Hurricane Hugo

1 measure vodka • 1 measure Amaretto
1 measure sloe gin • ½ measure Southern Comfort
½ measure Midori • 1 measure orange juice
1 measure cranberry juice

Batten down the hatches, its devastating! There are four measures of booze in this shot, so be prepared for a storm!

method

Put some ice cubes into the shaker. Using a jigger or shot glass, carefully measure out equal amounts of the ingredients and pour them into the shaker. Shake well and then strain into 6 shot glasses.

Inebriator

1 measure vodka • 1 measure Triple Sec
1 measure gin • 1 measure Amaretto
3 measures pineapple juice

Does exactly what it says on the label.
The pineapple juice and the almond-flavour of
the Amaretto can be deceptive – so go easy on
these shots!

method

Put some ice cubes into the shaker. Using a jigger or shot
glass, carefully measure out equal amounts of the
ingredients and pour them into the shaker. Shake and
then strain into 6 shot glasses.

Death By Sex

1 measure vodka • 1 measure Triple Sec
1 measure sloe gin • 1 measure peach schnapps
1 measure Amaretto • 1 measure Southern Comfort
½ measure cranberry juice • ½ measure orange

What a way to go! A real fruity confection, so you'll
'die' with a smile on your face.

method

Put some ice cubes into the shaker. Using a jigger or shot
glass, carefully measure out equal amounts of the
ingredients and pour them into the shaker. Shake and
then strain into 6 shot glasses. Say a prayer!

The Green Monster

1 measure vodka • 1 measure Cointreau
1 measure Midori • 1 measure peach schnapps
1 measure Southern Comfort

Remember the old adage: you are what you eat!
This beautiful delicately coloured shot is a power-
packed punch.

method

Put some ice cubes into the shaker. Using a jigger or shot
glass, carefully measure out equal amounts of the
ingredients and pour them into the shaker. Shake and
then strain into 6 shot glasses. If you turn into the
Incredible Hulk, it's your own fault – you've had one too
many shooters!

Jiggelos: Gelatine Shots

This is the basic recipe for 18-20 shots, which will happily serve 4 to 6 people. To make things simple in the recipes, we'll call the measure for the hot water 1 part, and the equivalent amount of spirits/liqueurs and/or juices 1 part.

- 1 packet jelly (see flavour combinations, or use unflavoured gelatine if you prefer shots that   are a little less sweet)
- hot water to dissolve the jelly: see the instructions on the package for the quantity
- the same quantity of your favourite spirit/liqueur and juices (or combination of spirits/liqueurs and juices) to make up the finished volume
- 20 disposable plastic shot glasses or disposable cups

Because of the different natures of spirits and liqueurs, some will set faster than others, so prepare your jiggelos well in advance of your party! Once you've got the hang of jiggelos, you can have real fun. You can make just about any cocktail or shooter recipe into a gelatine shot. You can layer them too: just let one level set in the fridge first before you add the next layer(s). If you want a clear level or layer in a jiggelo, then it's best to use unflavoured gelatine. Unflavoured gelatine gives you a neutral base which you can infuse with flavours from fresh juices and liqueurs, without adding any extra sweetness. The only liqueurs that don't work so well in jiggelos are the cream-based liqueurs such as Baileys Irish Cream, which tends to separate. However, while the visual effect may not be what you want, it won't affect the flavour.

Lemonhead

1 packet lemon-flavoured jelly • 1 part hot water to dissolve (see packet for quantity) • 1 part vodka

A citrus-vodka-flavoured jelly-shot that's easy to make and fun to eat.

method

In a heat-proof bowl, break or cut the lemon gelatine into cubes. Boil some water and measure out the quantity stated on the jelly packet required to dissolve the jelly. Stir until the jelly is dissolved. Let this mix cool. Pour in the vodka, an amount equal to the water, and stir to combine it well. Pour into plastic shot glasses or disposable cups and chill in the fridge until firm.

Berry Schnapps

1 packet strawberry-flavoured jelly
1 part hot water to dissolve (see packet for quantity)
1 part peach schnapps

Strawberries and peaches are perfect partners in this jiggelo, but you could try any of the variously flavoured schnapps to create your own versions.

method

In a heat-proof bowl, break or cut the strawberry gelatine into cubes. Boil some water and measure out the quantity stated on the jelly packet required to dissolve the jelly. Stir until the jelly is dissolved. Let this mix cool. Pour in the peach schnapps and stir to combine it well. Pour into plastic shot glasses or disposable cups and chill in the fridge until firm.

Jell-a-rita

1 packet lime-flavoured jelly • 1 part hot water to dissolve (see packet for quantity) • 1 part tequila

A jelly version of the famous tequila cocktail, the Margharita, created in 1948 by Danny Herrera for the actress Marjorie King, in Tijuana, Mexico.

method

In a heat-proof bowl, break or cut the lime gelatine into cubes. Boil some water and measure out the quantity stated on the jelly packet required to dissolve the jelly. Stir until the jelly is dissolved. Let this mix cool. Pour in the tequila and stir to combine it well. Pour into plastic shot glasses or disposable cups and chill in the fridge until firm.

Melon Sour

I packet lime-flavoured jelly • I part hot water to
dissolve (see packet for quantity) • I part Midori

Sours were drinks that first became popular in the
1850s. This jelly version uses one of the most recent
arrivals on the drink scene, Midori.

method

In a heat-proof bowl, break or cut the lime gelatine into
cubes. Boil some water and measure out the quantity
stated on the jelly packet required to dissolve the jelly.
Stir until the jelly is dissolved. Let this mix cool. Pour in
the Midori and stir to combine it well. Pour into plastic
shot glasses or disposable cups and chill in the fridge
until firm.

Tropical Orange

1 packet orange-flavoured jelly • 1 part hot water to dissolve (see packet for quantity) • 1 part Cointreau

Cointreau is a form of Triple Sec or a brandy-based liqueur flavoured with small, bitter oranges from the Caribbean island of Curacoa.

method

In a heat-proof bowl, break or cut the orange gelatine into cubes. Boil some water and measure out the quantity stated on the jelly packet required to dissolve the jelly. Stir until the jelly is dissolved. Let this mix cool. Pour in the Cointreau and stir to combine it well. Pour into plastic shot glasses or disposable cups and chill in the fridge until firm.

Tropical Rum

1 packet orange-flavoured jelly • 1 part hot water to dissolve (see packet for quantity) • 1 part Malibu

It was Christopher Columbus who took sugar cane to the Caribeean, where it was soon discovered that the sap made fine rum. This tropical jelly shot uses Malibu, a coconut-flavoured rum.

method

In a heat-proof bowl, break or cut the orange gelatine into cubes. Boil some water and measure out the quantity stated on the jelly packet required to dissolve the jelly. Stir until the jelly is dissolved. Let this mix cool. Pour in the Malibu and stir to combine it well. Pour into plastic shot glasses or disposable cups and chill in the fridge until firm.

Gimlet

1 packet lime-flavoured jelly • 1 part hot water to dissolve (see packet for quantity) • 1 part gin

A 'gimlet' is a small, sharp hand tool used to bore holes in wood. The word has also become associated with small, sharp-tasting cocktails.

method

In a heat-proof bowl, break or cut the lime gelatine into cubes. Boil some water and measure out the quantity stated on the jelly packet required to dissolve the jelly. Stir until the jelly is dissolved. Let this mix cool. Pour in the gin, an amount equal to the water and stir to combine it well. Pour into plastic shot glasses or disposable cups and chill in the fridge until firm.

Wobbly Mimosa

I packet orange-flavoured jelly
I part hot water to dissolve (see packet for quantity)
I part flat champagne or flat sparkling white whine

Champagne or sparkling wine lost its fizz? Turn it into a jiggelo!

method

In a heat-proof bowl, break or cut the orange gelatine into cubes. Boil some water and measure out the quantity stated on the jelly packet required to dissolve the jelly. Stir until the jelly is dissolved. Let this mix cool. Pour in the flat champagne or white wine and stir to combine it well. Pour into plastic shot glasses or disposable cups and chill in the fridge until firm.

Sherry Trifle

1 packet strawberry-flavoured jelly
1 part hot water to dissolve (see packet for quantity)
1 part dry sherry • Whipped cream

Sherry is too often overlooked as a drink, so here's a perfect solution: a 'pudding' shot!

method

In a heat-proof bowl, break or cut the strawberry gelatine into cubes. Boil some water and measure out the quantity stated on the jelly packet required to dissolve the jelly. Stir until the jelly is dissolved. Let this mix cool. Pour in the sherry and stir to combine it well. Pour into plastic shot glasses or disposable cups and chill in the fridge until firm. Top each shot with a dollop of whipped cream if you like!

Flat Tyre, Inflated

1-2 envelopes unflavoured gelatine (enough to make 18-20 shots, see packs for quantities) • 1 part hot water to dissolve (see packet for quantity) • ½ part tequila • ½ part Sambuca

We met the original flat tyre earlier on. Now try it inflated, as a jiggelo!

method

Following the instructions on the package for quantities and methods, dissolve the gelatine with the appropriate amount of hot water and stir well to dissolve. Let this cool. When cool, measure out the tequila and Sambuca. The total amount of these should equal the amount of hot water used to dissolve the gelatine. Mix together the tequila and Sambuca. Shake with a few ice cubes if you like, then strain and pour into the gelatine mix. Stir well to combine, then pour into individual shot glasses and chill in the fridge until firm.

Wobbling Green Beret

1-2 envelopes unflavoured gelatine (enough to make 18-20 shots, see packs for quantities) • 1 part hot water to dissolve (see packet for quantity) • ½ part vodka • ½ part green crème de menthe

A jelly version of this minty shooter!

method

Following the instructions on the package for quantities and methods, dissolve the gelatine with the appropriate amount of hot water and stir well to dissolve. Let this cool. When cool, measure out the vodka and green crème de menthe. The total amount of these should equal the amount of hot water used to dissolve the gelatine. Mix together the vodka and green crème de menthe. Shake with a few ice cubes if you like, then strain and pour into the gelatine mix. Stir well to combine, then pour into individual shot glasses and chill in the fridge until firm.

Mexican Jumping Jelly Bean

1-2 envelopes unflavoured gelatine (enough to make 18-20
shots, see packs for quantities)
1 part hot water to dissolve (see packet for quantity)
½ part Kahlua • ½ part tequila • Good splash of Grenadine

Jump for joy after tasting this
Mexican delight.

method

Following the instructions on the package for quantities
and methods, dissolve the gelatine with the appropriate
amount of hot water and stir well to dissolve. Let this
cool. When cool, measure out the tequila and Kahlua. The
total amount of these should equal the amount of hot
water used to dissolve the gelatine. Mix together the
tequila and Kahlua. Shake with a few ice cubes if you like,
then strain and pour into the gelatine mix. Stir well to
combine, then pour into individual shot glasses and chill
in the fridge until firm.

Slow Comfortable French Jelly Bean

1-2 envelopes unflavoured gelatine (enough to make 18-20 shots, see packs for quantities)
1 part hot water to dissolve (see packet for quantity)
2 part sloe gin • ½ part Pernod • ½ part Southern Comfort

Slow from sloe gin; comfortable from Southern Comfort; French from Pernod.

method

Following the instructions on the package for quantities and methods, dissolve the gelatine with the appropriate amount of hot water and stir well to dissolve. Let this cool. When cool, measure out the sloe gin, Pernod and Southern Comfort. The total amount of these should equal the amount of hot water used to dissolve the gelatine. Mix together the sloe gin, Pernod and Southern Comfort. Shake with a few ice cubes if you like, then strain and pour into the gelatine mix. Stir well to combine, then pour into individual shot glasses and chill in the fridge until firm.

Italian Jelly Bean

1-2 envelopes unflavoured gelatine (enough to make
18-20 shots, see packs for quantities)
1 part hot water to dissolve (see packet for quantity)
⅓ part sambuca • ⅓ part Galliano • ⅓ part Grenadine

The Italians in here are Sambuca and Galliano – with
a little Grenadine added for good measure!

method

Following the instructions on the package for quantities
and methods, dissolve the gelatine with the appropriate
amount of hot water and stir well to dissolve. Let this
cool. When cool, measure out the sambuca, Galliano, and
Grenadine. The total amount of these should equal the
amount of hot water used to dissolve the gelatine. Mix
together the sambuca, Galliano and Grenadine. Shake
with a few ice cubes if you like, then strain and pour into
the gelatine mix. Stir well to combine, then pour into
individual shot glasses and chill in the fridge until firm.

Bean There, Done That!

Tequila and Amaretto are a surprisingly fine combination.

method

Following the instructions on the package for quantities and methods, dissolve the gelatine with the appropriate amount of hot water and stir well to dissolve. Let this cool. When cool, measure out the tequila, Amaretto and Grenadine. The total amount of these should equal the amount of hot water used to dissolve the gelatine. Mix together the tequila, Amaretto and Grenadine. Shake with a few ice cubes if you like, then strain and pour into the gelatine mix. Stir well to combine, then pour into individual shot glasses and chill in the fridge until firm.

Tricoleurs

Layered jelly shots take a bit of forward planning as you need to chill and set each layer before you add the next one. You can have great fun adding as many different layers, colours and flavours as you like. They're great for big parties: if you make up enough recipe of each colour to make 20 shots, you'll actually be able to make around sixty 3-layered shots! But make sure you've got room in your fridge first! Alternatively, follow the instructions on the gelatine packet regarding quantities/amounts and adjust according to the number of shots you require in total.

Red, White & Blue

Red layer (bottom): 1-2 envelopes unflavoured gelatine (enough to make 18-20 shots, see packs for quantities) • 1 part hot water to dissolve (see packet for quantity) • 1 part Grenadine or sloe gin

method

Following the instructions on the package for quantities and methods, dissolve the gelatine with the appropriate amount of hot water and stir well to dissolve. Let this cool. Pour in the Grenadine or sloe gin and stir well. Pour the gelatine mix into the shot glass to fill ⅓ of the glass. Chill in the fridge until firm.

White layer (middle): 1-2 envelopes unflavoured gelatine (enough to make 18-20 shots, see packs for quantities) • 1 part hot water to dissolve (see packet for quantity) • 1 part vodka or Cointreau

method

Make up the gelatine mix, add the vodka or Cointreau and stir. Pour on top of the firmly set Grenadine or sloe gin layer to fill the glass ⅔ full. Place back in the fridge to chill and set.

Blue layer (top): 1-2 envelopes unflavoured gelatine (enough to make 18-20 shots, see packs for quantities) • 1 part hot water to dissolve (see packet for quantity) • 1 part blue curacao

method

Make up the gelatine mix, add the blue curacao and stir. Pour on top of the firmly set clear vodka or Cointreau layer. Place back in the fridge to chill and set.

Red, Gold & Green

Red layer (bottom): 1-2 envelopes unflavoured gelatine (enough to make 18-20 shots, see packs for quantities) • 1 part hot water to dissolve (see packet for quantity) • 1 part Grenadine

method Following the instructions on the package for quantities and methods, dissolve the gelatine with the appropriate amount of hot water and stir well to dissolve. Let this cool. Pour in the Grenadine and stir well. Pour the gelatine mix into the shot glass to fill ⅓ of the glass. Chill in the fridge until firm.

Gold layer (middle): 1-2 envelopes unflavoured gelatine (enough to make 18-20 shots, see packs for quantities) • 1 part hot water to dissolve (see packet for quantity) • 1 part gold tequila or Galliano

method Make up the gelatine mix, add the gold tequila or Galliano and stir. Pour on top of the firmly set Grenadine layer to fill the glass ⅔ full. Place back in the fridge to chill and set.

Green layer (top): 1-2 envelopes unflavoured gelatine (enough to make 18-20 shots, see packs for quantities) • 1 part hot water to dissolve (see packet for quantity) • 1 part Midori

method Make up the gelatine mix, add the Midori and stir. Pour on top of the firmly set gold tequila layer to fill the glass. Place back in the fridge to chill and set.

Double Chocolate Mint Stick

Bottom layer: 1–2 envelopes unflavoured gelatine (enough to make 18–20 shots, see packs for quantities) • 1 part milk to dissolve (see packet for quantity and replace the water with an equal amount of milk) • 1 part dark crème de cacao

method

Add the gelatine to the milk and whisk well. Let the mix sit for 2–3 minutes before bringing it to the boil over a medium heat, whisking frequently to dissolve the gelatine. Let the mixture cool for 10 minutes before adding the dark crème de cacao. Stir to mix. Pour into glasses to fill them ⅓ full and set in the fridge to chill and firm.

Middle layer: 1–2 envelopes unflavoured gelatine (enough to make 18–20 shots, see packs for quantities) • 1 part milk to dissolve 1 part green crème de menthe

method

Follow the instructions for the first layer. When the milk and gelatine mix is cool, add the green crème de menthe and stir to mix. Pour on top of the first layer, up to the ⅔ level and put back in the fridge to set.

Top layer: 1–2 envelopes unflavoured gelatine (enough to make 18–20 shots, see packs for quantities) • 1 part milk to dissolve 1 part white crème de cacao

method

Follow the instructions as for the first two layers. When the milk and gelatine mix is cool, add the white crème de cacao and stir to mix. Pour this final layer on top of the middle layer, and set back in the fridge to chill and set.

Bibliography

Peter Bohrmann **The Bartenders Guide** *Greenwich Editions, 2004*

Mary Breidenbach, Barrett J. Calhoon & Sharon L. Calhoon
Jiggelo: Inventive Gelatin Shots for Creative Imbibers *Ten Speed Press, 2004*

David Briggs **The Cocktail Handbook** *New Holland, 1999*

Salvatore Calabrese **Classic Cocktails** *Prion, 1997*

Maria Costantino **The Cocktail Handbook** *Silverdale Books*

Maria Costantino **Cocktails Deluxe** *Silverdale Books*

Dale DeGroff **The Craft of the Cocktail** *Clarkson Potter, 2002*

David A. Embury **The Fine Art of Mixing Drinks** *Faber, 1963*

Robert Cross **The Classic 1000 Cocktail Recipes** *Foulsham, 2003*

Peter Raymond Foley **The Ultimate Cocktail Book** *Foley, 1999*

Ambrose Heath **Good Drinks** *Faber, 1939*

Mattie Hellmich **Party Shots: Recipes for Jiggle-iscious Fun** *Chronicle Books, 2003*

Michael Jackson **Michael Jackson's Bar & Cocktail Book** *Mitchell Beazley, 2002*

Michael Jackson **Michael Jackson's Pocket Bar Book** *Mitchell Beazley, 1981*

Paul Knorr **Big Book of Bad-ass Shots** *Running Press, 2004*

Brian Lucas **365 Cocktails** *Duncan Baird, 2003*

Harry MacElhone with Andrew MacElhone **Harrys ABC of Mixing Cocktails**
Souvenir Press, 1986

Gary Regan **The Bartender's Bible** *Harper Collins, 1993*

Ian Wisniewski **Party Cocktails** *Conran Octopus, 2002*

Check out the web for cocktail related sites.

Drink databases and Cocktail Sites:

www.kingcocktail.com
Dale DeGroff, acknowledged as the one of the world's, if not the world's greatest living bartenders. Learn more about bartending, the art of mixology, classes and recipes at this terrific site.

www.cocktails.about.com
A terrific site, newsletter, history, recipes, trivia and party games!

www.barback.com
Paul Knorr's huge recipe collection!

www.cocktails.com
A great site with recipes and links to Cocktail Communiqué and other interesting sites.

www.cocktaildb.com
Martin Doudroff's and Ted (Dr Cocktail) Haigh's extensive database of recipes, and a great message board too!

Newsletters and Cocktail Chat:

www.ardentspirits.com
A free newsletter by noted authors Gary and Mardee Regan. Just send them your e-mail address!

cocktailcommunique@yahoogroups.co.
The weekly publication of cocktails.com

www.spiritjournal.com
F. Paul Pacult's quarterly newsletter covering wines and beers as well as spirits.

Classes and Seminars:

www.ipbartenders.com
www.ukbg.co.uk (The United Kingdom Chapter of the Bartenders Guild)
www.wset.co.uk (The Wine and Spirit Education Trust)
www.cockatil.uk (A full-service site: equipment, classes, seminars and recipes!)

Remember: Please drink responsibly!

Index

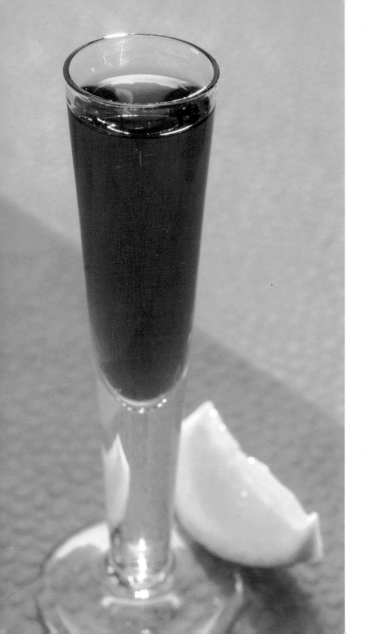

Credits

Paul Forrester for photography.

Eva for the use of her kitchen, fridge and for lunch!

Jo Locke for being a great neighbour and for her valiant
(and unfaltering) taste testings.